SECOND EDITION

Volume II

HAL LEONARD EUROPE
DISTRIBUTED BY MUSIC SALES

Exclusive Distributors:
Music Sales Limited
14-15 Berners Street, London W1T 3LJ, UK.

Order No. HLE90003782
ISBN: 978-1-84772-990-3

Your Guarantee of Quality
As publishers, we strive to produce every book to the highest commercial standards. The book has been carefully designed to minimise awkward page turns and to make playing from it a real pleasure. Throughout, the printing and binding have been planned to ensure a sturdy, attractive publication which should give years of enjoyment. If your copy fails to meet our high standards, please inform us and we will gladly replace it.

www.musicsales.com

PREFACE

The Real Book is the answer to the fake book. It is an alternative to the plethora of poorly designed, illegible, inaccurate, badly edited volumes which abound on the market today. The Real Book is extremely accurate, neat, and is designed, above all, for practical use. Every effort has been made to make it enjoyable to play. Here are some of the primary features:

1. FORMAT

a. The book is professionally copied and meticulously checked for accuracy in melody, harmony, and rhythms.

b. Form within each tune, including both phrases and larger sections, is clearly delineated and placed in obvious visual arrangement.

c. All two-page tunes open to face one another.

d. Most standard-type tunes remain true to their original harmonies with little or no reharmonisation. The exceptions include a handful of jazz interpretations of popular songs and Broadway showtunes, as well as some modifications using modern notation and variation among turnarounds.

2. SELECTION OF TUNES AND EDITING

a. Major jazz composers of the last 60 years are highlighted, with special attention given to the 1960s and 1970s.

b. While some commonly played tunes are absent from the book, many of the classics are here, including bop standards and a fine selection of Duke Ellington masterpieces. See The Real Book Volume 1 for more tunes.

c. Many of the included arrangements represent the work of the jazz giants of the last 40 years – Miles, Coltrane, Shorter, Hancock, Rollins, Silver, and Monk, as well as a variety of newer artists.

d. A variety of recordings and alternate editions were consulted to create the most accurate and user-friendly representations of the tunes, whether used in a combo setting or as a solo artist.

3. SOURCE REFERENCE

a. The composer(s) of every tune is listed.

b. Every song presented in The Real Book is now fully licensed for use.

Second Edition

This new edition contains tunes that are re-arranged, re-transcribed and most importantly, licensed, so that you may study and play these works more accurately and legally. Enjoy!

M

N

O

P

Q

R

S

T

U

W

Y

(♩=192 (MED. UP)

ABLUTION

-LENNIE TRISTANO

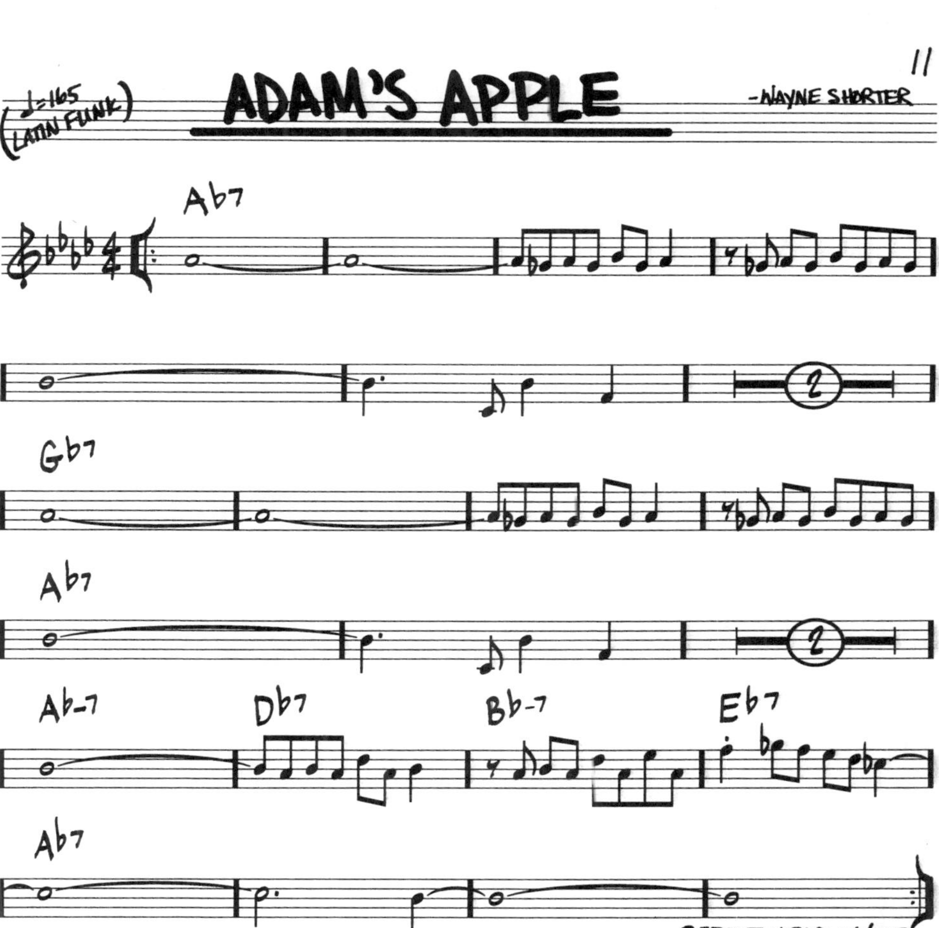
ADAM'S APPLE
♩=165
(LATIN FUNK)
-WAYNE SHORTER
Ab7
Gb7
Ab7
Ab-7
Db7
Bb-7
Eb7
Ab7
REPEAT HEAD IN/OUT

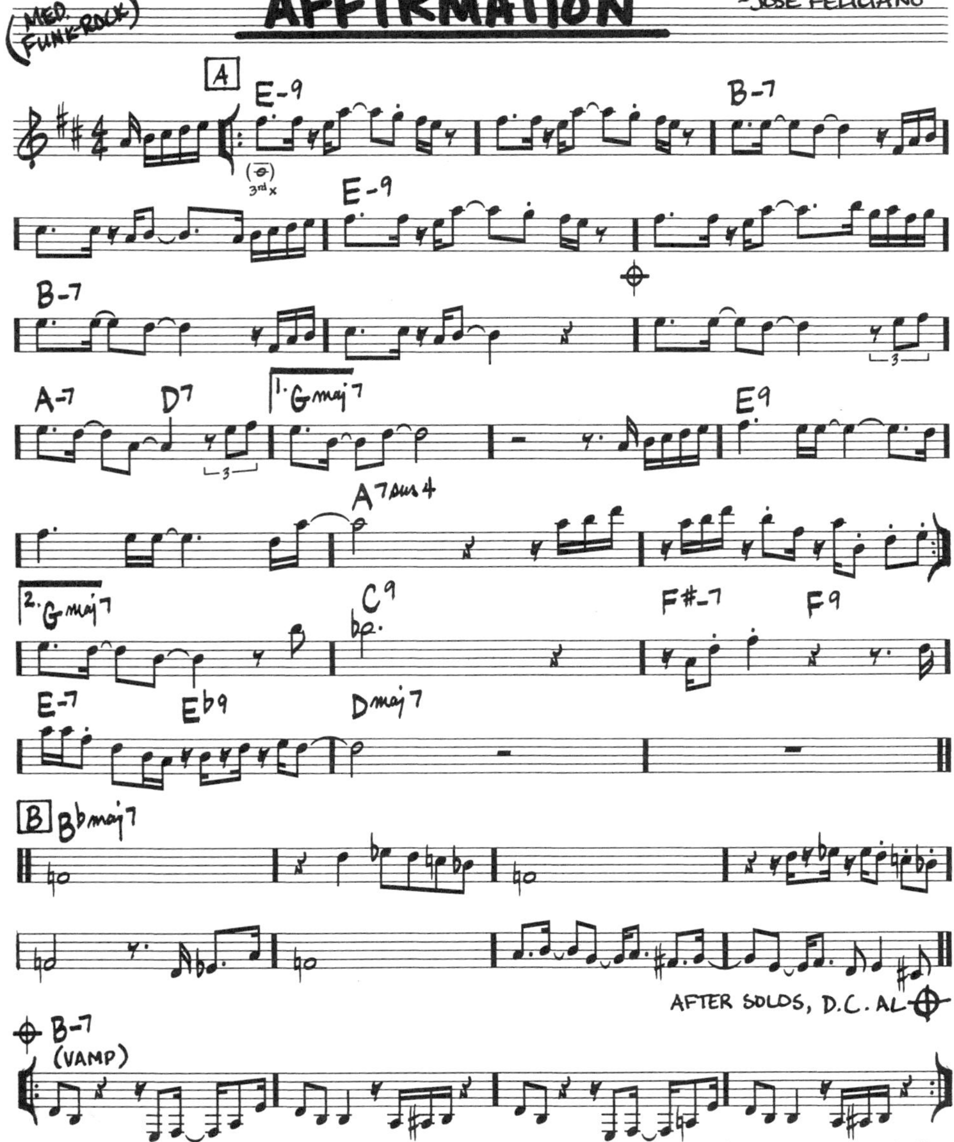
(MED. FUNK-ROCK)
AFFIRMATION
-JOSÉ FELICIANO
A
E-9
B-7
3rd x
E-9
B-7
A-7
D7
1. Gmaj7
E9
A7sus4
2. Gmaj7
C9
F#-7
F9
E-7
Eb9
Dmaj7
B
Bbmaj7
AFTER SOLOS, D.C. AL
B-7
(VAMP)
REPEAT AND FADE

(SWING)

ALFIE'S THEME

—SONNY ROLLINS

ALL ALONE (LEFT ALONE)

(BALLAD)

–BILLIE HOLIDAY / MAL WALDRON

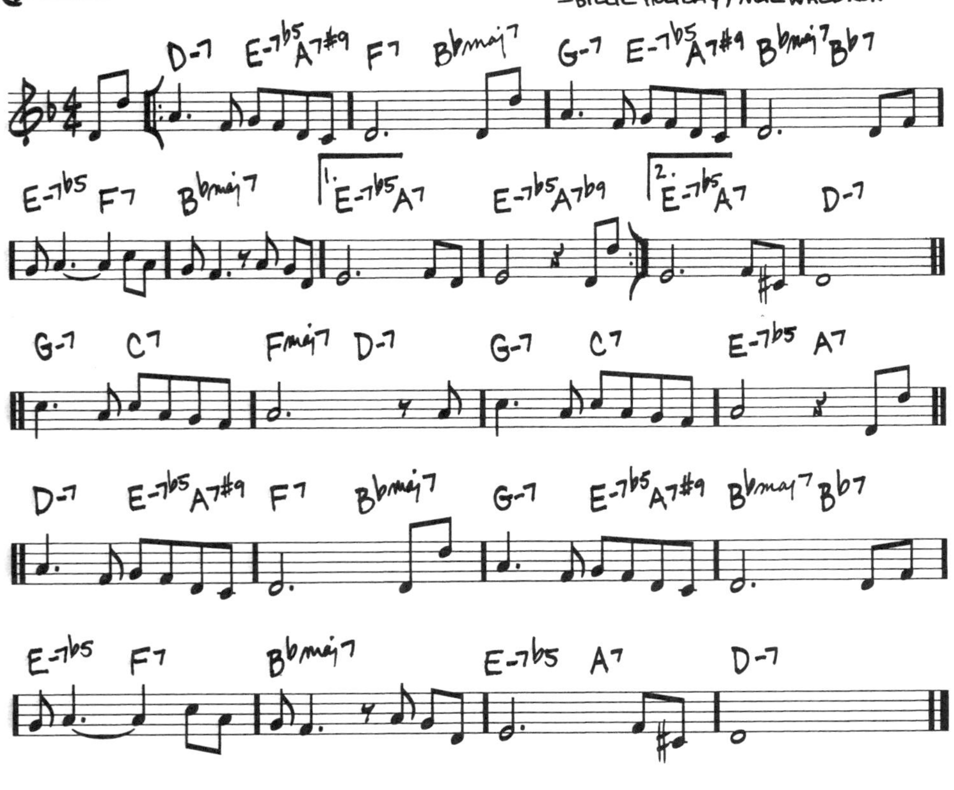

(BALLAD)

ALL MY TOMORROWS

– JAMES VAN HEUSEN/
SAMMY CAHN

ALONG CAME BETTY
(MED. SWING)
-BENNY GOLSON
Bb-7 B-7 E7 Bb-7 B-7 E7
Amaj7 G#7 Gmaj7 F#7
F#-7 G-7 C7 F#-7 G-7 C7
Fmaj7 A7 D-7 G7
C-7 F7b9 A-7b5 D7b9 G-7 G-7/F
E-7b5 A7 F-7 Bb7
Bb-7 B-7 E7 Bb-7 B-7 E7
C-7b5 F7b9 Bb-7b5 Eb7#9
Abmaj7 (B-7 E7)

ALTO ITIS

-Oliver E. Nelson

(UP)

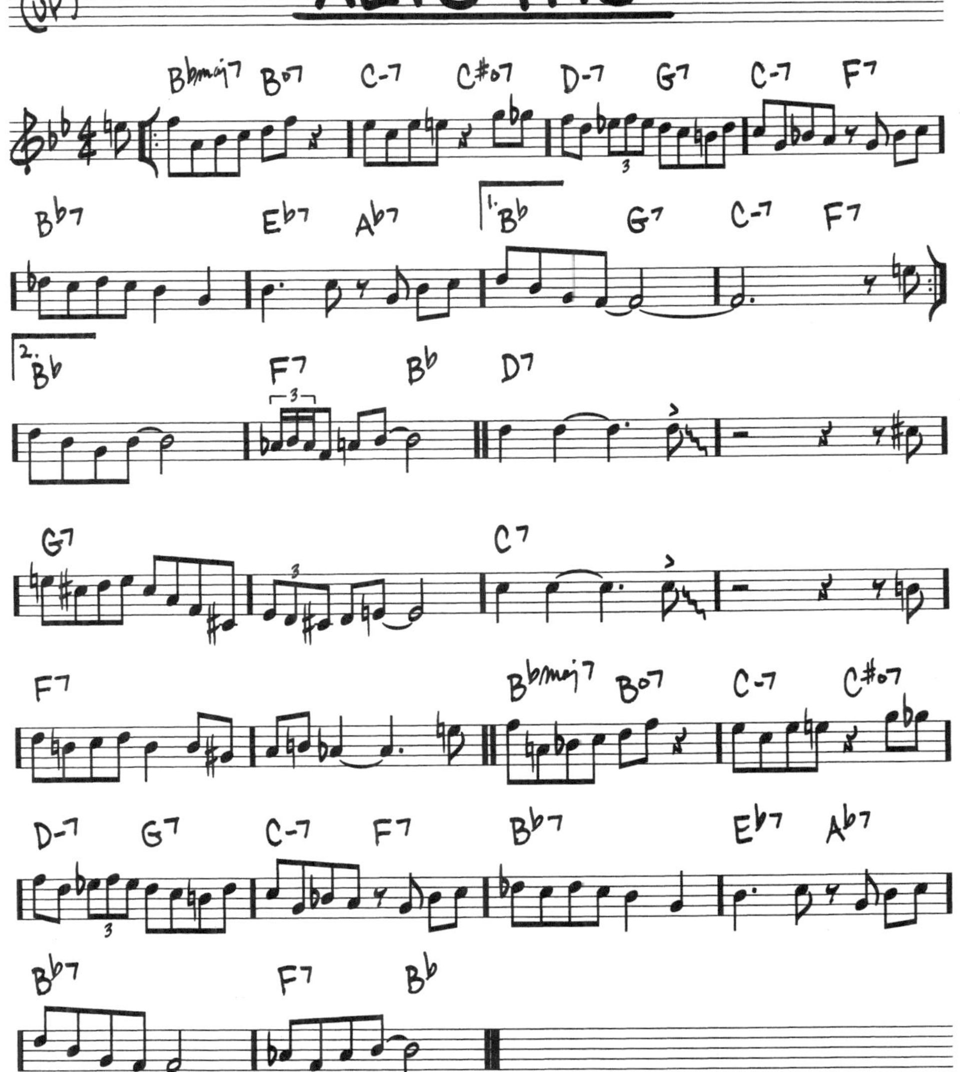

APRIL SKIES

(MED. UP)

—BUDDY COLLETTE

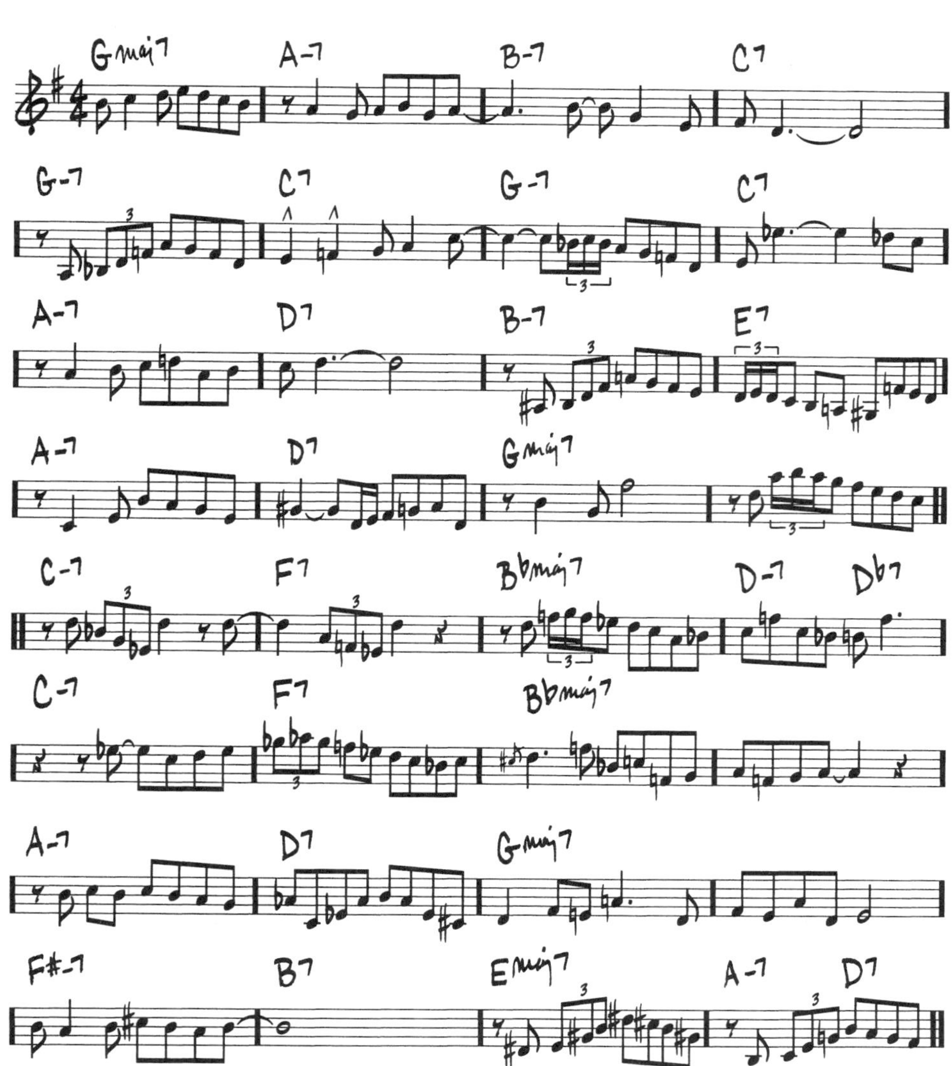

Gmaj7
A-7
B-7
C7
G-7
C7
G-7
C7
A-7
D7
B-7
E7
A-7
D7
Gmaj7
E7
A-7
D7
AFTER SOLOS, D.C. AL
Gmaj9

AQUELLOS OJOS VERDES

(GREEN EYES)

(MED. LATIN)

-NILO MENENDEZ/ADOLFO UTRERA/E.RIVERA/E.WOODS

Ebmaj7 Eb6 Ebmaj7

Eb6 Eo7 F-7 Bb7

F-7 Bb7 F-7 Bb7

Db9 C9 F7 Bb7

Ebmaj7 Eb6 Ebmaj7

G-7b5 C7 F-7 C7 F-7

Ab-6 Ao7 Eb/Bb Db9 C9

F7 F-7 Bb7 Eb6 (F-7 Bb7)

ASK ME NOW
(WALKING BALLAD)
—THELONIOUS MONK
G-7 C7 F#-7 B7 F-7 Bb7 E-7 A7 Eb-7 Ab7#5
B7b5 Bb7 Eb7 D7 Dbmaj7 Eb7
1. Eb-7 Ab7b9 B7b5 Bb7b5 A7b5 Ab7b5 2. Eb-7 Ab7b9 Db6
Eb-7 Ab7 Dbmaj7 Eb-7 D9 Dbmaj7
Eb7 Eb-7/Ab Ab7b9
Gb7 G-7 C7 F#-7 B7 F-7 Bb7 E-7 A7
Eb-7 Ab7#5 B7b5 Bb7 Eb7 D7
Dbmaj7 Eb7 Eb-7 Ab7b9 Db6

(MAMBO)

AT THE MAMBO INN

- GRACE SAMPSON/
BOBBY WOODLEN/
MARIO BAUZA

AZURE

–Duke Ellington

(Med. Slow Swing)

F#/G G | G F#/G | F#/G G A- D7 | Gmaj7

F#/G G | G F#/G | F#/G G A- D7 | Gmaj7 G7

B C D6 D#o7 | E- D-7 G7 | B C G/D G | A7 D7

F#/G G | G F#/G | F#/G G A- D7 | Gmaj7

(MED. BLUES)

BA-LUE BOLIVAR BA-LUES-ARE
(BOLIVAR BLUES)

-THELONIOUS MONK

(MED.)

BABY, IT'S COLD OUTSIDE

-FRANK LOESSER

CAN ALSO BE PLAYED "CALL AND RESPONSE" STYLE WITH ADDITIONAL MELODY INSTRUMENT

(MED. BLUES)
BAGS AND TRANE
-MILT JACKSON
INTRO
N.C.
(UNISON)
(MELODY)
HEAD
C-7
F-7
C-7
Ab7
G7#5
1. C-7
2. C-7
(SOLO BREAK)

BAGS' GROOVE

(MED. SWING)

-MILT JACKSON

28
BAIA
(BAHIA)
(MED. BOSSA)
-ARY BARROSO/
RAY GILBERT
INTRO
Eb7
INTRO RIFF
HEAD
Eb7
W/ INTRO RIFF
Abmaj7
Db9#11
G-7
C7b9
F-7
Bb7(#9)
Eb7
REPEAT HEAD IN/OUT

BALI HA'I

(MED. BALLAD)

– RICHARD RODGERS/
OSCAR HAMMERSTEIN II

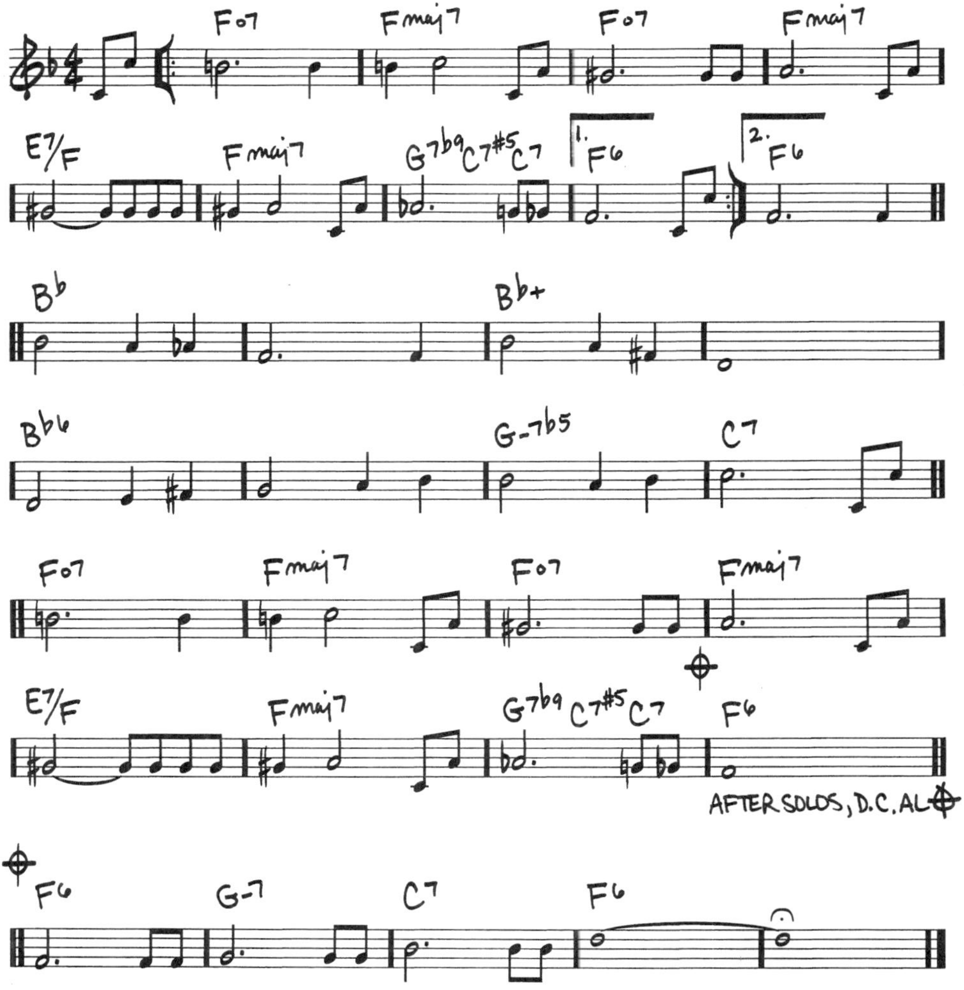

F°7 Fmaj7 F°7 Fmaj7

E7/F Fmaj7 G7b9 C7#5 C7 1. F6 2. F6

Bb Bb+

Bb6 G-7b5 C7

F°7 Fmaj7 F°7 Fmaj7

E7/F Fmaj7 G7b9 C7#5 C7 F6

AFTER SOLOS, D.C. AL ⊕

⊕ F6 G-7 C7 F6

A BALLAD

(SLOW)

-GERRY MULLIGAN

Dbmaj7 E-7 A7 D-7 G7b9 Cmaj7
C#-7 F#7#9 Bmaj7 E-7 A7#5 G-7b5 F#-7 B7b9
E-7 A7b9 F#-7 B7b9 E-7 G-6 F#-7 Fo7
E-7 A7b9 Dmaj7
(ENDING)
D-7 G7 E-7 A7#9 D7b9 Ab7 Abo7 A07 Bb7 Bo7 C Dbmaj9 Cmaj9

BARBARA
(JAZZ WALTZ)
– HORACE SILVER
Bb7b9
Ab7b9
Ab7b9
Bb7b9
Bb-7/Eb
Ab-7
Db7
Gbmaj7
1.
F-7
Bb7
G-7
C7b9
F-7
Bb7b9
2.
F-7
Bb7
G-7
C7b9
F#-7
B7
F-7
Bb7
Ebmaj7
Dbmaj7
Bmaj7
Dbmaj7
Ebmaj7
Dbmaj7
Bmaj7
Dbmaj7

BE-BOP
-John "Dizzy" Gillespie
(Fast Bop)
INTRO
F- C7 F- Bb7 F- C7 F-
N.C.
HEAD
F- G°7 F-/Ab Bb-6
F-/C G-7b5 C7 F- G°7 F-/Ab Bb-6
1. F-/C G-7b5 C7 F- 2. F-/C G-7b5 C7 F-
F-7 Bb7 Eb6
Eb-7 Ab7 Db6 G-7b5 C7b5
F- G°7 F-/Ab Bb-6 F-/C G-7b5 C7
F- G°7 F-/Ab Bb-6 F-/C G-7b5 C7 F-

(MED.)

THE BEST THINGS IN LIFE ARE FREE

-B.G. DeSYLVA/LEW BROWN/RAY HENDERSON

BIG P

JIMMY HEATH

(FAST SWING)

D-7 E/D Eb/D | D-7 | D7#9

G-7 A/G Ab/G | D-7 | / / B-7b5

Bb7 | A7#9 | D-7 | E-7b5 A7b9

D-7 | E/D Eb/D | D-7 | D7#9

G-7 | A/G Ab/G | D-7 | / / B-7b5

Bb7 | A7#9 | D-7 | (E-7b5 A7b9)

[SOLOS ON D- BLUES]

BILL'S HIT TUNE

(MED.)

-BILL EVANS

BILLIE'S BLUES
(I LOVE MY MAN)

(SLOW BLUES)

—BILLIE HOLIDAY

Ab Db7 Ab Ab7

Db7 Ab

Bb-7 Eb7 Ab Db7 1. Ab Eb7

2. Ab Eb7 Ab N.C. Ab N.C. Ab N.C.

Ab7 Db7 Ab

Bb-7 Eb7 Ab Db7

Ab Eb7 AFTER SOLOS, D.C. AL ⊕ (TAKE 2nd ENDING)

⊕ Ab A7 Ab7

BIRD FEATHERS

(BOP)

-CHARLIE PARKER

(SLOW SWING) THE BIRTH OF THE BLUES

—RAY HENDERSON/B.G. DE SYLVA/LEW BROWN

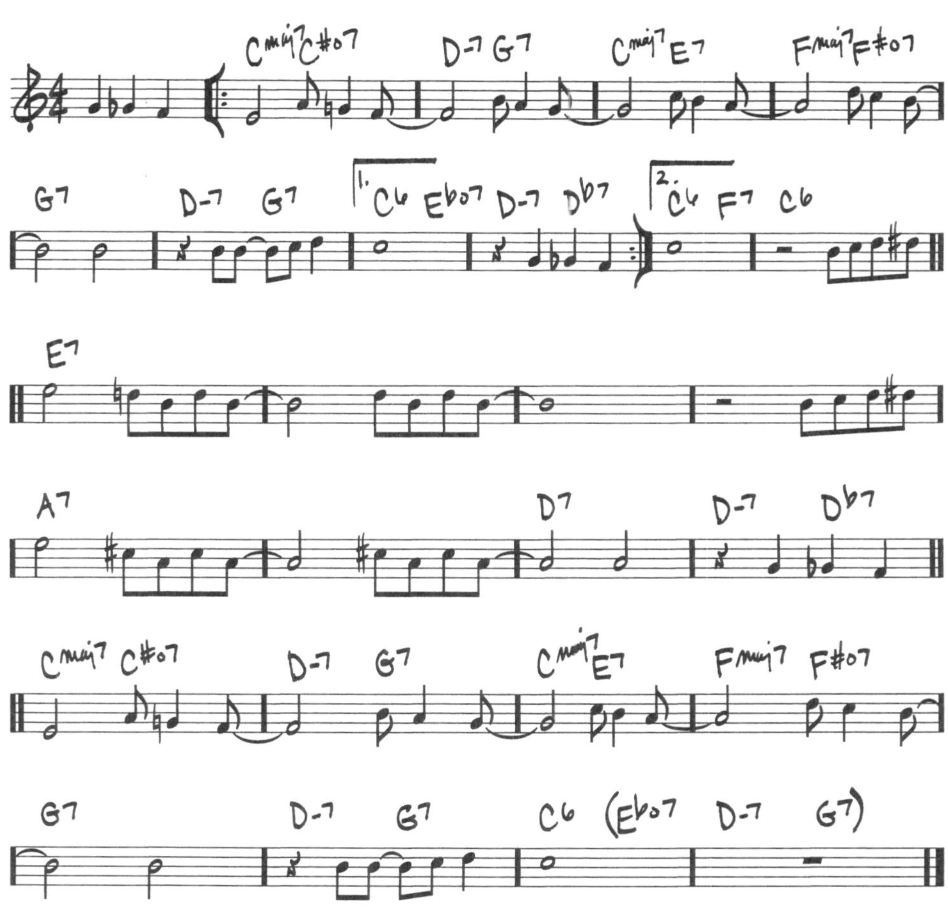

MED. (EVEN 8THS)
BIRDLAND
-JOSEF ZAWINUL
INTRO
N.C.
1., 2.
3.
(BASS)
A
* 8VA
1., 2., 3.
4.
G-
* 3rd, 4th TIMES ONLY
B
(G-) F/G F/Bb Eb/Bb D-7 F/C C-7 F/B E- G-/C
(G-/C) F/Eb E- F Gb G E- G-/C F/C G
C
(G PEDAL)
1. – 4.
5.

D G C G
G C G B-7b5
G7 (FUNK) 7
E G B- E- G/B Cmaj7 C#-7b5 B-7 E7
A-7 G/B C6 C/D G B- E- C6 C#-7b5 D-7 Cmaj7 A-7 Cmaj7/E A-7/D G
(G) B- E- G/D C#-7b5 C9 B- E7 A- G/B C6 C/D G B- E- A-7/D
(A-7/D) C#-7b5 C9 B-7 E7 A- G/B C6 C/D
F G7 (G PEDAL) 19 G7
(G7) Gb7 F7 E7 Eb7 D7 Db7 C7 G7 Gb7 F7 E7 Eb7 D7 Db7 C7 G 3
PLAY 6X
D.S. TO A, TAKE REPEATS
PLAY THROUGH C, GO TO E
REPEAT AND FADE ON E

BITCHES BREW

-MILES DAVIS

(BALLAD)

BLACKBERRY WINTER

-ALEC WILDER/LOONIS McGLOHON

(MED.)

THE BLESSING

—ORNETTE COLEMAN

BLOOMDIDO

(FAST BLUES)

—CHARLIE PARKER

46
(BALLAD)
A BLOSSOM FELL
-HOWARD BARNES/
HAROLD CORNELIUS/
DOMINIC JOHN
Bb6 B°7 C-7
F7 F7#5 Bb6 Bbmaj7 Bb/D Db°7
C-7 F7 C-7 F7 F7#5 Bb6 B°7 F7/C F7
Bb6 B°7 C-7 F7 F7#5
Bbmaj7 Bb7#5 Ebmaj7 Bbmaj7
C-7 F7 F-7 Bb7 Bb7#5 Ebmaj7 Eb-6
Bb/D Db°7 C-7 F7 Bb6 (C-7 F7)

(BOP)
BLUE 'N BOOGIE
- JOHN "DIZZY" GILLESPIE/
FRANK PAPARELLI

B♭6
3
3

E♭7
3
3
B♭6

C-7
3
F7
3
B♭6

BLUE SERGE

—MERCER ELLINGTON

(MED. BLUES)

BLUE SEVEN

—SONNY ROLLINS

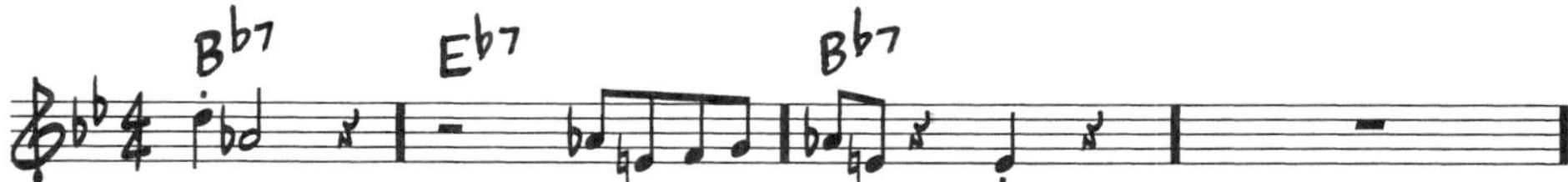

F7 Eb7 Bb7 F7

Blue Silver

(Med.)

—Horace Silver

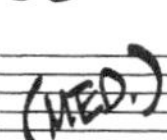

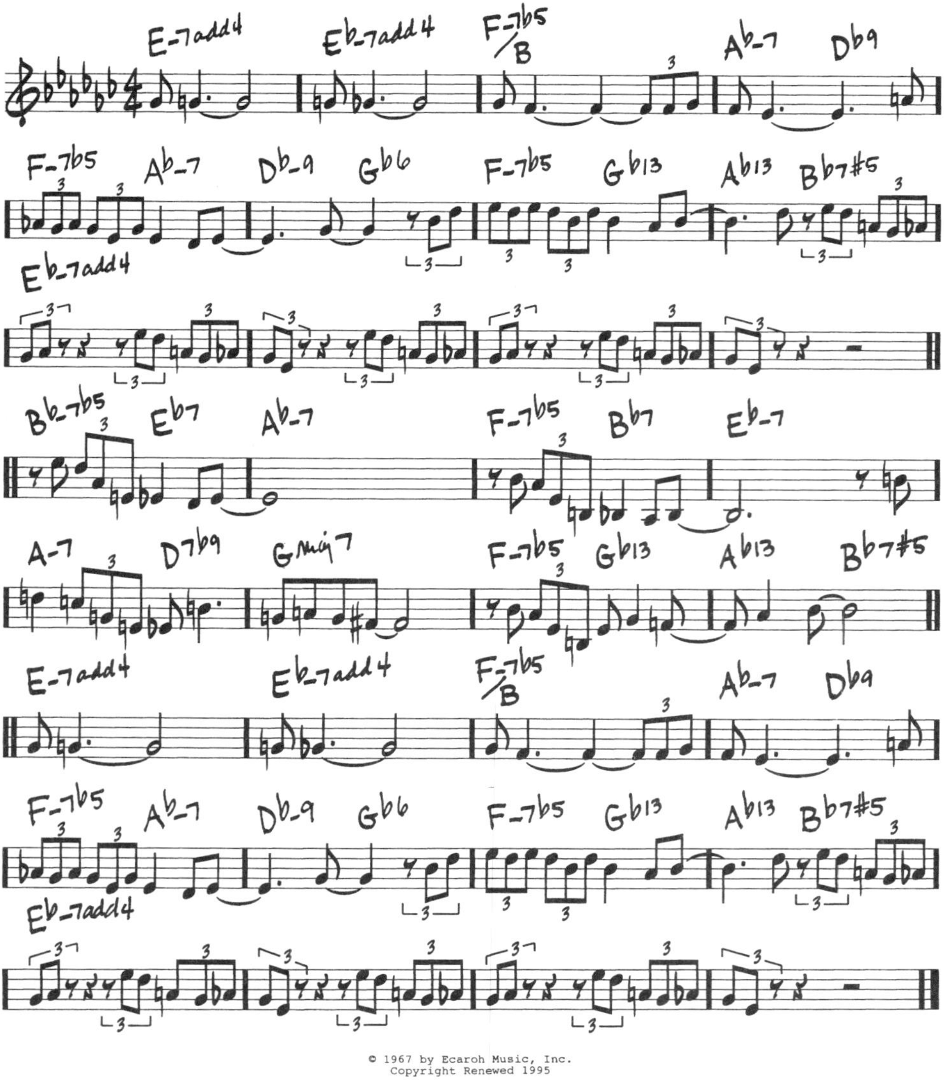
E-7add4
Eb-7add4
F-7b5/B
Ab-7
Db9
F-7b5
Ab-7
Db-9
Gb6
F-7b5
Gb13
Ab13
Bb7#5
Eb-7add4
Bb-7b5
Eb7
Ab-7
F-7b5
Bb7
Eb-7
A-7
D7b9
Gmaj7
F-7b5
Gb13
Ab13
Bb7#5
E-7add4
Eb-7add4
F-7b5/B
Ab-7
Db9
F-7b5
Ab-7
Db-9
Gb6
F-7b5
Gb13
Ab13
Bb7#5
Eb-7add4

BLUES BY FIVE

— RED GARLAND

(MED. FAST)

Bb7

2.
C-7 F7

BLUES FOR WOOD

(MED. FAST)

– WOODY SHAW

(BRIGHT BLUES)

BLUES IN THE CLOSET

-OSCAR PETTIFORD

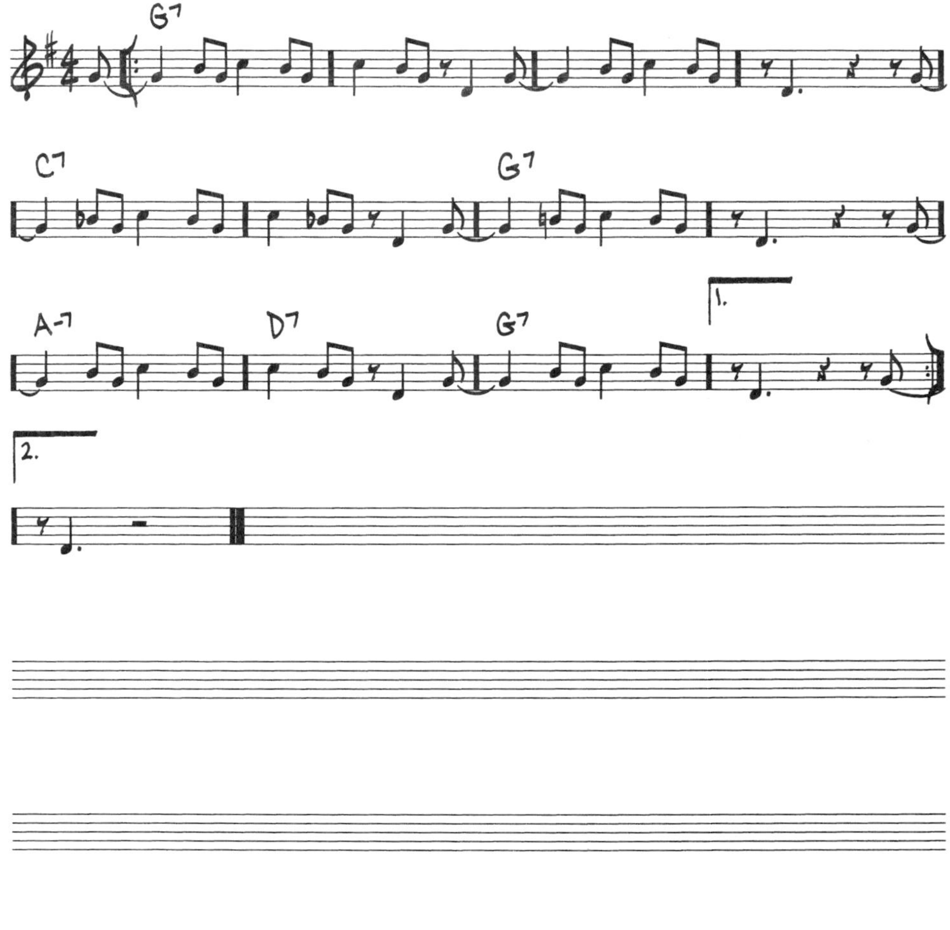

(MED. FAST)

BOHEMIA AFTER DARK

—OSCAR PETTIFORD

G- A-7b5 D7 G- A-7b5 D7

G- A-7b5 D7 G- 1. Eb7 D7 G- D7 2. (G-)

(MED-UP SWING)

BOLIVIA

— CEDAR WALTON

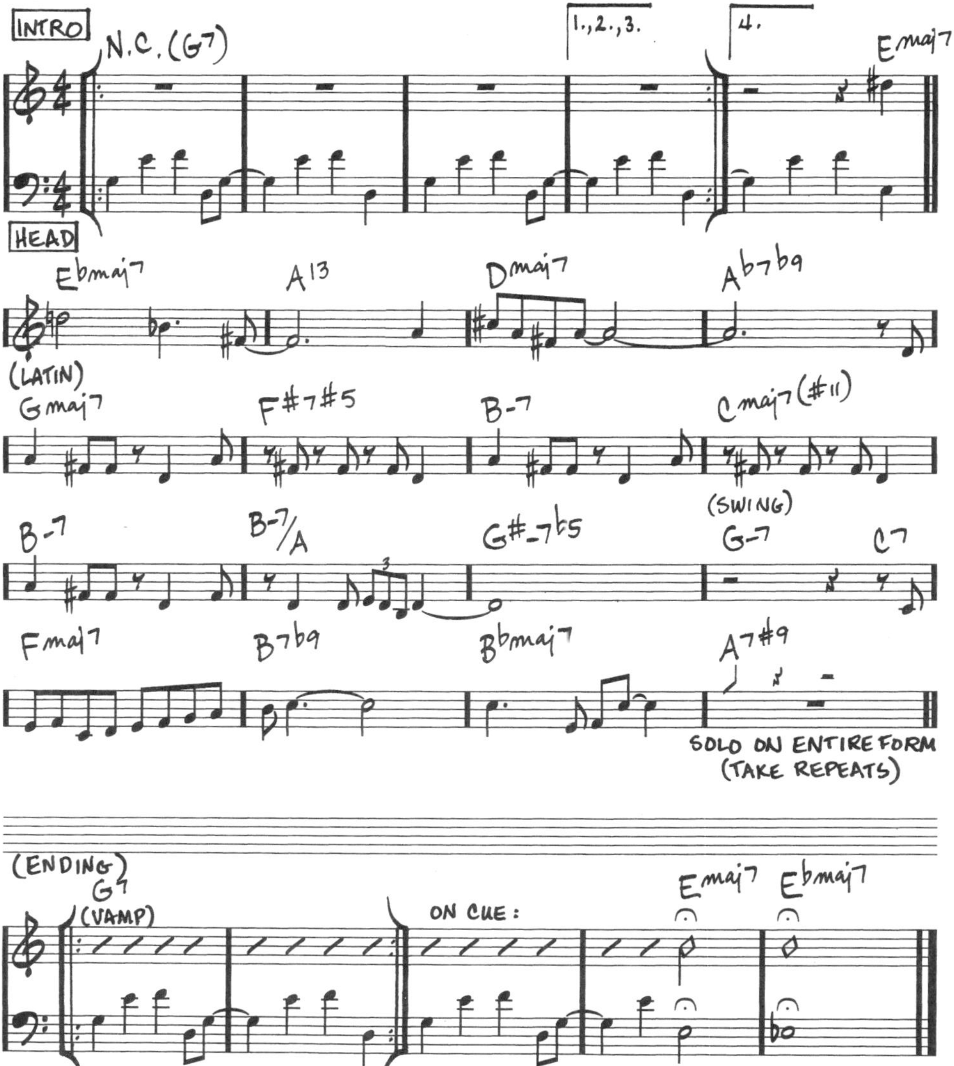
INTRO
N.C. (G7)
1.,2.,3.
4.
Emaj7
HEAD
Ebmaj7
A13
Dmaj7
Ab7b9
(LATIN)
Gmaj7
F#7#5
B-7
Cmaj7(#11)
B-7
B-7/A
G#-7b5
(SWING)
G-7
C7
Fmaj7
B7b9
Bbmaj7
A7#9
SOLO ON ENTIRE FORM
(TAKE REPEATS)
(ENDING)
G7
(VAMP)
ON CUE:
Emaj7
Ebmaj7

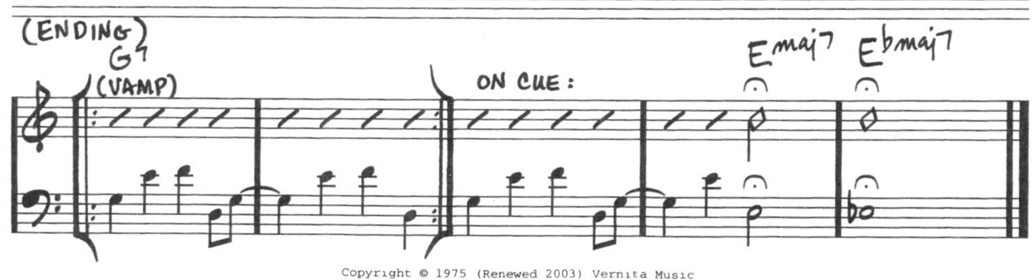

(BALLAD)

BORN TO BE BLUE

– ROBERT WELLS/ MEL TORME

BOSSA ANTIGUA

- PAUL DESMOND

(MED. FAST ♩=95)

Bb-7 Eb7 C-7 F-7

Bb-7 Eb7 C-7 F7

Bb-7 Eb7 C-7 F-7

Bb-7 D-7 G7 Cmaj7 A-7

D-7 G7 E-7 A-7

D-7 G7 C-7 F7

Bb-7 Eb7 C-7 F-7

Bb-7 Eb7 Abmaj7

(MED.-UP SWING)
BOUNCING WITH BUD
-EARL BUD POWELL/WALTER GIL FULLER
INTRO
Bbmaj7
B7b5
1.
2.
A
Bbmaj7 C-7 D-7 Eb-7 D-7 G7 C-7 D7
G-7 C#o7 C-7 F7 Bbmaj7 F7b5
Bbmaj7 C-7 D-7 Ebmaj7 D-7 G7 C-7 D7
G-7 C#o7 C-7 F7 Bbmaj7 D7
B
G- A-7b5 D7#5(#9)
G7 F7 C-7 F7#5

C Bbmaj7 C-7 D-7 Eb-7 D-7 G7 C-7 D7

G-7 C#o7 C-7 F7 Bbmaj7

FINE

D D7/F# G- D7 G- Bo7 C-7 G7 C-7 Gb7

F7

(FILL)

B7 Bb6

(SOLO BREAK)

SOLO A B C

AFTER SOLOS, D.C. AL FINE

(RHUMBA)

THE BREEZE AND I

– ERNESTO LECUONA
AL STILLMAN

BRIGHT BOY

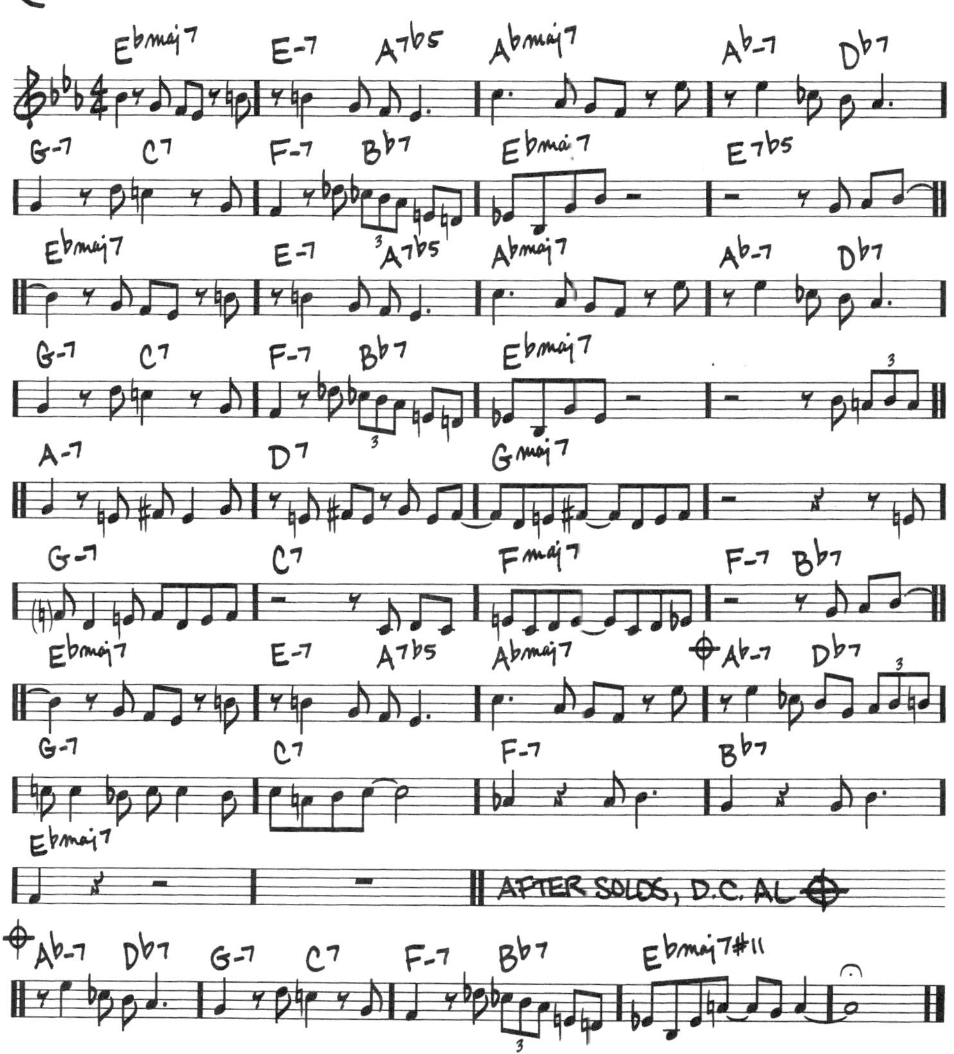
(MED.-UP SWING)
BRIGHT BOY
-JOHN BRIGHT
Ebmaj7
E-7
A7b5
Abmaj7
Ab-7
Db7
G-7
C7
F-7
Bb7
E7b5
A-7
D7
Gmaj7
Fmaj7
Ebmaj7#11
AFTER SOLOS, D.C. AL

BRILLIANT CORNERS

–THELONIOUS MONK

1st TIME: SLOW WALK, EVEN 8ths
ON REPEAT: MED.-UP SWING

BUSTER RIDES AGAIN

—EARL "BUD" POWELL

(SWING)

E♭7 B♭7 E♭7 B♭7

E♭7 B♭7 1. G♭7 F7

2. G♭7 F7 B♭7

BYE BYE BLACKBIRD

(MED. UP)

–RAY HENDERSON/MORT DIXON

CARAVAN
(BRIGHT AFRO-LATIN)
-DUKE ELLINGTON
A (LATIN)
C7
Db7
C7
Db7
C7
Db7
C7
F-6
FINE
B (SWING)
F7
Bb7
Eb7
Ab6
C7
D.C. AL FINE
SOLO A A B A

66
CALDONIA
(WHAT MAKES YOUR BIG HEAD SO HARD?)
MED. SWING BLUES
—FLEECIE MOORE
INTRO
C7
F7
C7
D-7
G7
C7
C7
F7
C7
D-7
G7
C7

[SOLOS ON C BLUES]

CAREFUL

(MED. EVEN 8THS)

– JAMES S. HALL

(MED. FUNK)

CHAMELEON

– HERBIE HANCOCK/ PAUL JACKSON/ HARVEY MASON/ BENNIE MAUPIN

CHASIN' THE TRANE

(FAST BLUES)

—JOHN COLTRANE

COLD DUCK TIME

(MED. ROCK)

— EDDIE HARRIS

(MED. JAZZ WALTZ)

CIRCLE

— MILES DAVIS

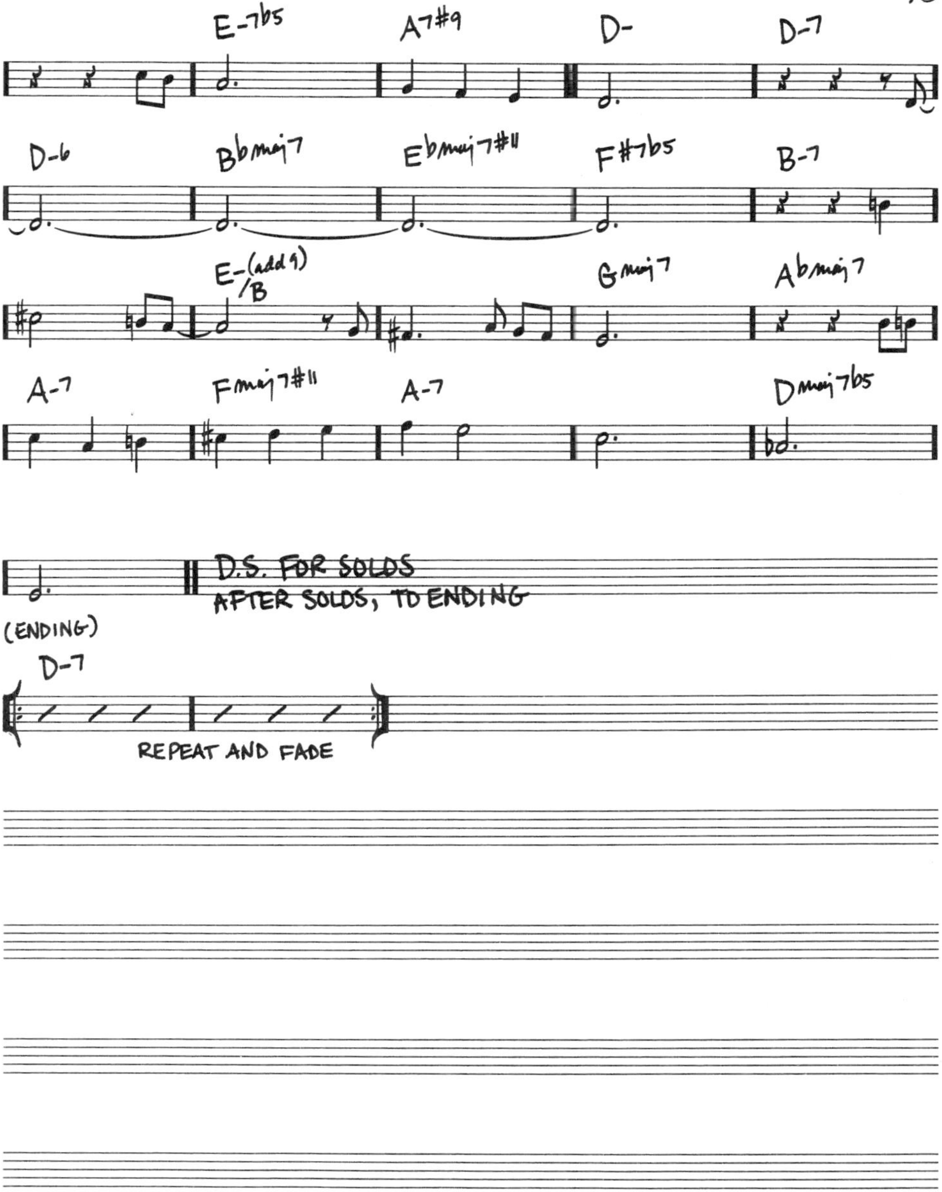
E-7b5
A7#9
D-
D-7
D-6
Bbmaj7
Ebmaj7#11
F#7b5
B-7
E-(add 9)/B
Gmaj7
Abmaj7
A-7
Fmaj7#11
A-7
Dmaj7b5
D.S. FOR SOLOS
AFTER SOLOS, TO ENDING
(ENDING)
D-7
REPEAT AND FADE

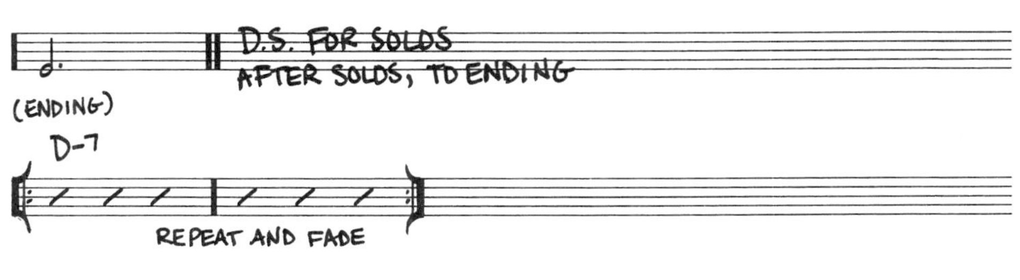

COMIN' HOME BABY

(SOUL JAZZ)

– BOB DOROUGH/ BEN TUCKER

CONTINUUM

(ROCK)

-JACO PASTORIUS

(BRIGHT BLUES)

—CHARLIE PARKER

C

F7 C

D-7 G7 C

THE CORE

(MED. SWING)

-FREDDIE HUBBARD

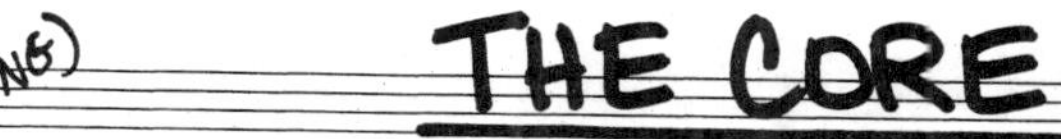

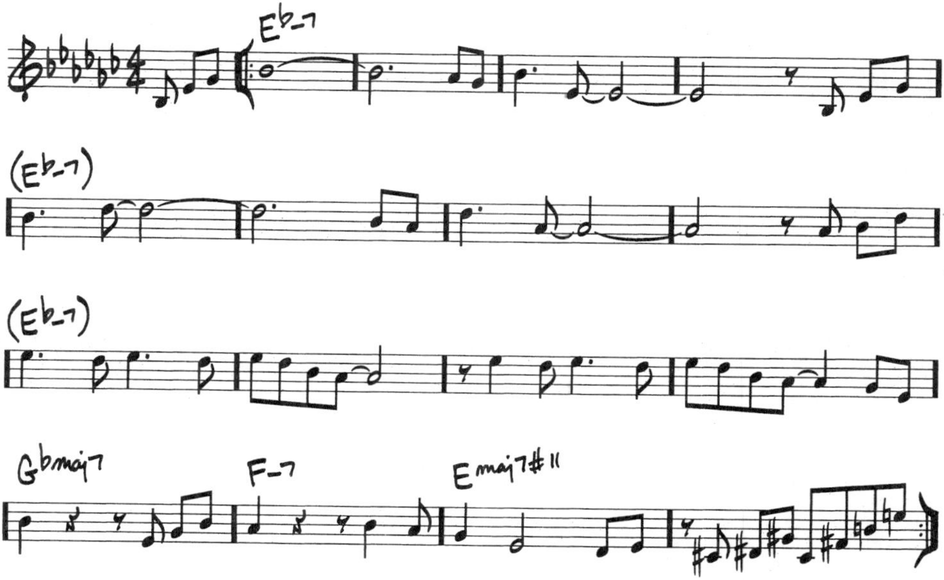
E♭-7
(E♭-7)
(E♭-7)
G♭maj7
F-7
Emaj7♯11

(MED.)

A COTTAGE FOR SALE

-WILLARD ROBISON/LARRY CONLEY

(UP)

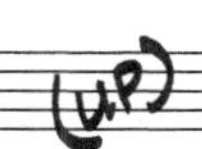

COUSIN MARY

-JOHN COLTRANE

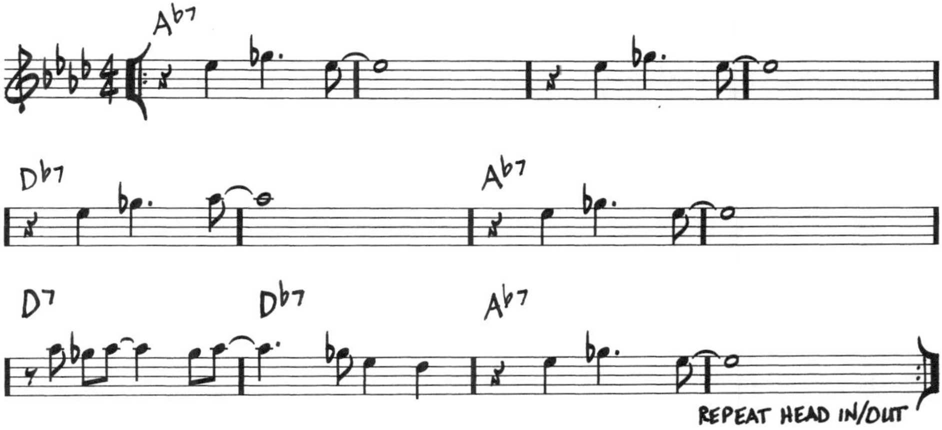
Ab7
Db7
Ab7
D7
Db7
Ab7
REPEAT HEAD IN/OUT

(BALLAD)

CRAZY SHE CALLS ME

– BOB RUSSELL / CARL SIGMAN

(MED. SLOW SWING)

THE CREOLE LOVE CALL

-DUKE ELLINGTON

Bbmaj7

Bb7

Ebmaj7

Bbmaj7

F7 C-7 F7 Bb6 Ebmaj7

1. Bbmaj7 2. Bbmaj7

[SOLOS ON Bb BLUES]

(MED. SWING)
CRISS CROSS
-THELONIOUS MONK
G- Gb7#9 Bb7
D- G7 G7b5 Gb7(13)
C-7 F7 Bb C-7
F7 Bb Gb7
G- Gb7#9 Bb7
D- G7 G7b5 Gb7(13) (Gb7b9)
(LAST X)
FINE

(BOP)
DANCE OF THE INFIDELS
-EARL "BUD" POWELL
F6 Bb-7 Eb7 A-7 G-7 F#-7 B7
F-7 Bb7 A-7 Ab-7 Db7
G-7 Db-7 Gb7 F6
C PEDAL
1.
2.
SOLOS
F6 Bb-7 Eb7 A-7 G-7 F#-7 B7
F-7 Bb7 A-7 Ab-7 Db7
G-7 Db-7 Gb7 F6 C7#5

DAY BY DAY

–SAMMY CAHN/
AXEL STORDAHL/
PAUL WESTON

(MED.)

(BALLAD)
DAY DREAM
– DUKE ELLINGTON/
BILLY STRAYHORN/
JOHN LATOUCHE

'DEED I DO

—WALTER HIRSCH/
FRED ROSE

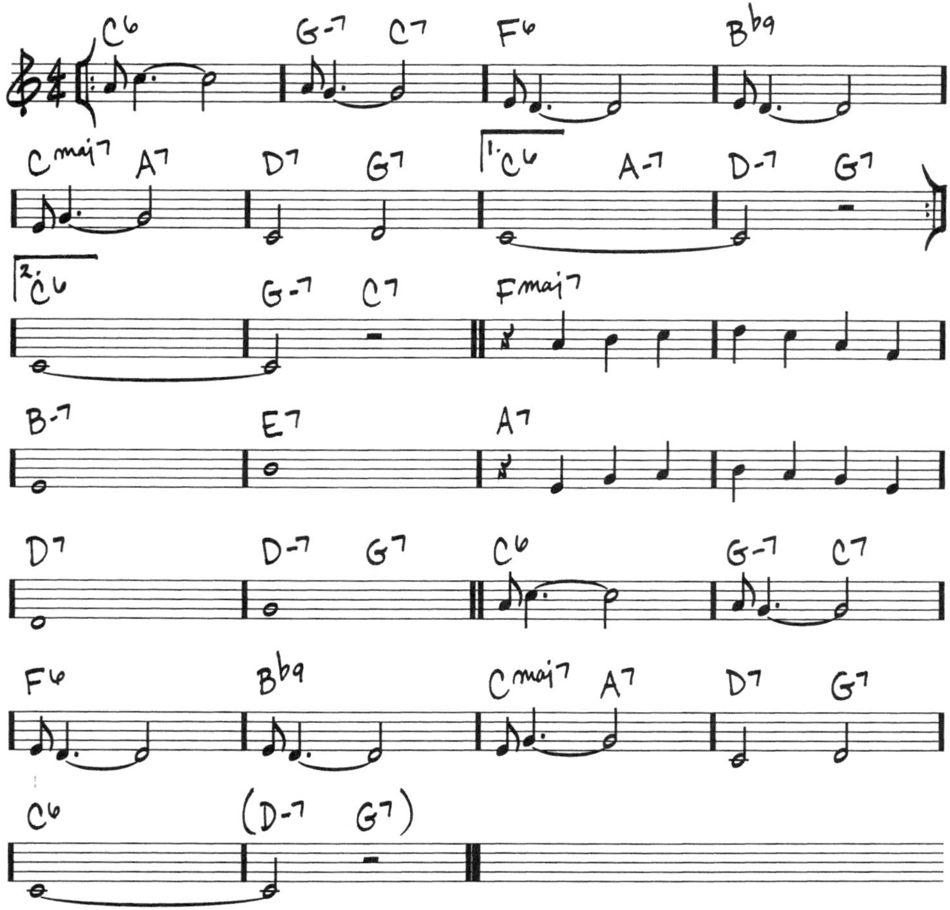

C6 G-7 C7 F6 B♭9
Cmaj7 A7 D7 G7 1. C6 A-7 D-7 G7
2. C6 G-7 C7 Fmaj7
B-7 E7 A7
D7 D-7 G7 C6 G-7 C7
F6 B♭9 Cmaj7 A7 D7 G7
C6 (D-7 G7)

(BOP)

DEWEY SQUARE

— CHARLIE PARKER

DIG
(MED. UP SWING)
-MILES DAVIS
F7
Bb7
Eb7
Abmaj7
G-7
C7
F7
Bb7
F-7
C7
F-7
Abmaj7
F7
Bb-7
Eb7
Ab6

(SLOW BOSSA)

DINDI

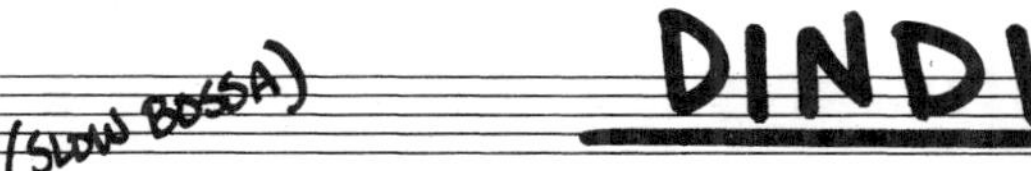

-ANTONIO CARLOS JOBIM/
ALOYSIO DE OLIVEIRA/
RAY GILBERT

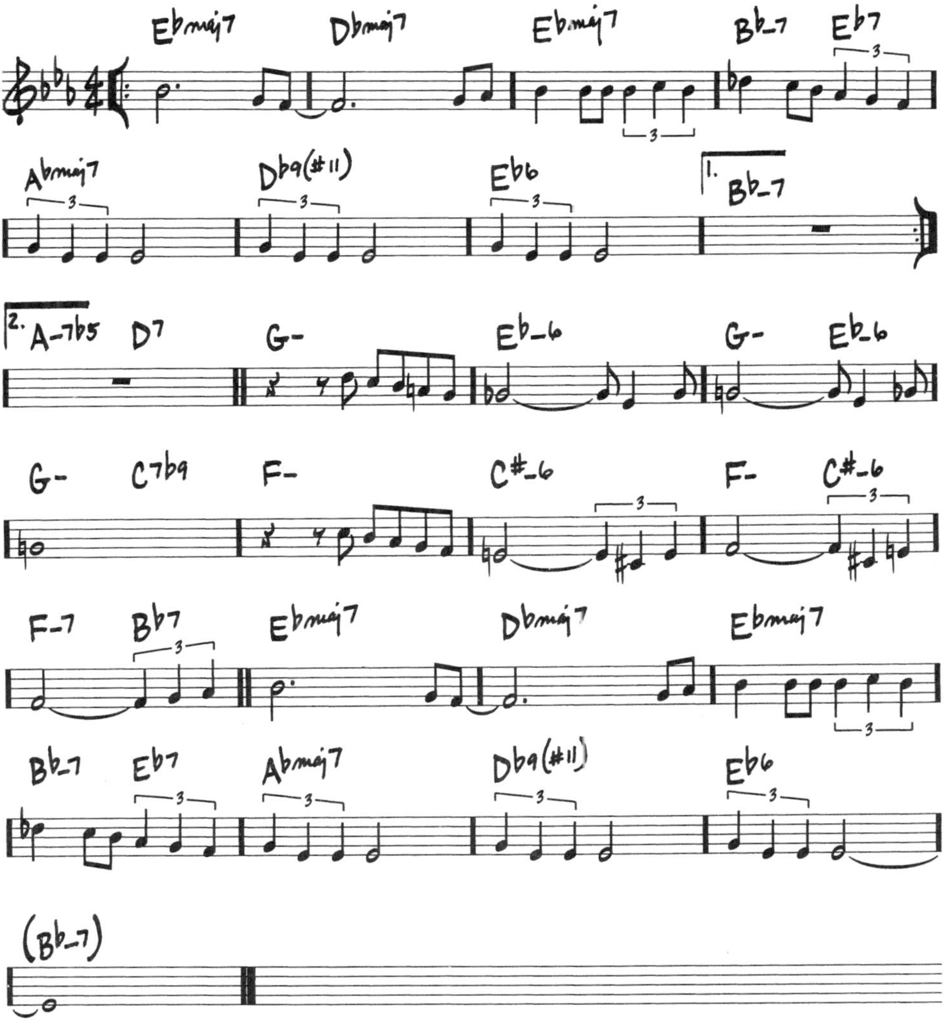

Ebmaj7 Dbmaj7 Ebmaj7 Bb-7 Eb7
Abmaj7 Db9(#11) Eb6 1. Bb-7
2. A-7b5 D7 G- Eb-6 G- Eb-6
G- C7b9 F- C#-6 F- C#-6
F-7 Bb7 Ebmaj7 Dbmaj7 Ebmaj7
Bb-7 Eb7 Abmaj7 Db9(#11) Eb6
(Bb-7)

(MED.) DO I LOVE YOU BECAUSE YOU'RE BEAUTIFUL?

-RICHARD RODGERS/OSCAR HAMMERSTEIN II

DON'T EVER GO AWAY
(POR CAUSA DE VOCE)

(BOSSA)

- ANTONIO CARLOS JOBIM / RAY GILBERT / DOLORES DURAN

Bbmaj7 Bb6 | Bbmaj7 Bb7 | Eb6/Bb | Eb-6/Bb

C-7 Ab-6 | C-7 F7 | D-7 D-7b5/Ab | G7

Ebmaj7 Eb6 | E-7b5 A7 | D-7 Bb-6 | D-7b5 G7

C-7 Ab-6 | C-7 F7 | Bbmaj7 | D-7b5 G7

C-7 C-7/Bb | A-7b5 F7 | Bbmaj7 | D-7b5 G7

C-7 Ab-6 | C-7 F7 | D-7b5 | G7b5 G7

Ebmaj7 Eb6 | E-7b5 C-7b5 | Bbmaj7 D7/A | G7 G7#5

C-7 | C-7b5 F7 | Bb6 | (C-7 F7)

DON'T EXPLAIN

(BALLAD)

-BILLIE HOLIDAY/
ARTHUR HERZOG

(BALLAD)

DON'T WORRY 'BOUT ME

-RUBE BLOOM/TED KOEHLER

DOXY

-SONNY ROLLINS

(MED.)

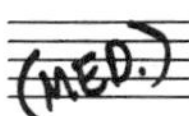

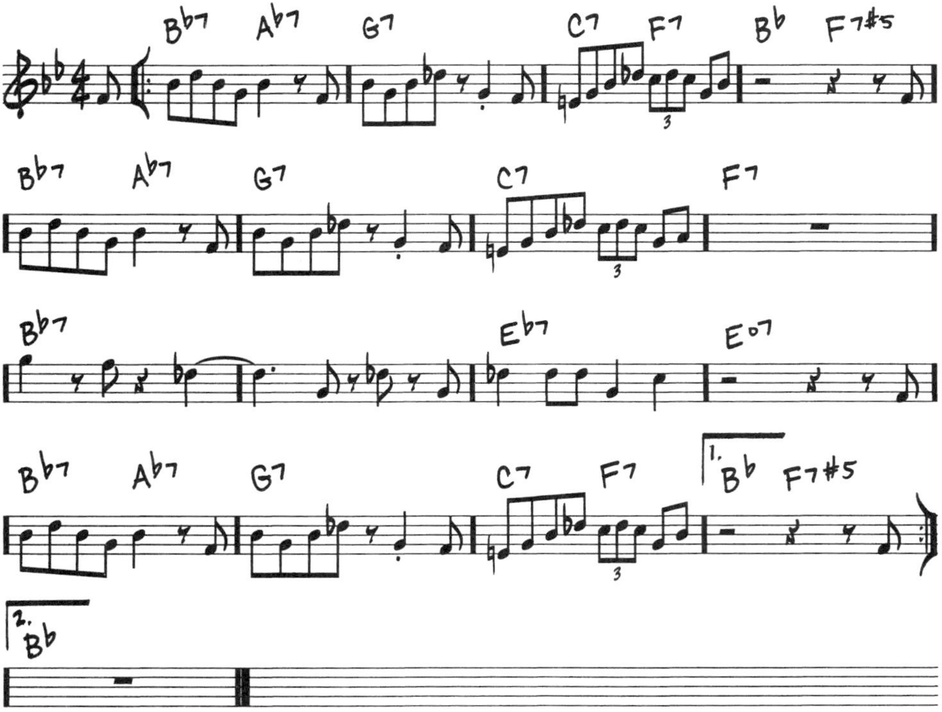
Bb7 Ab7 G7 C7 F7 Bb F7#5
Bb7 Ab7 G7 C7 F7
Bb7 Eb7 E°7
Bb7 Ab7 G7 C7 F7
1. Bb F7#5
2. Bb

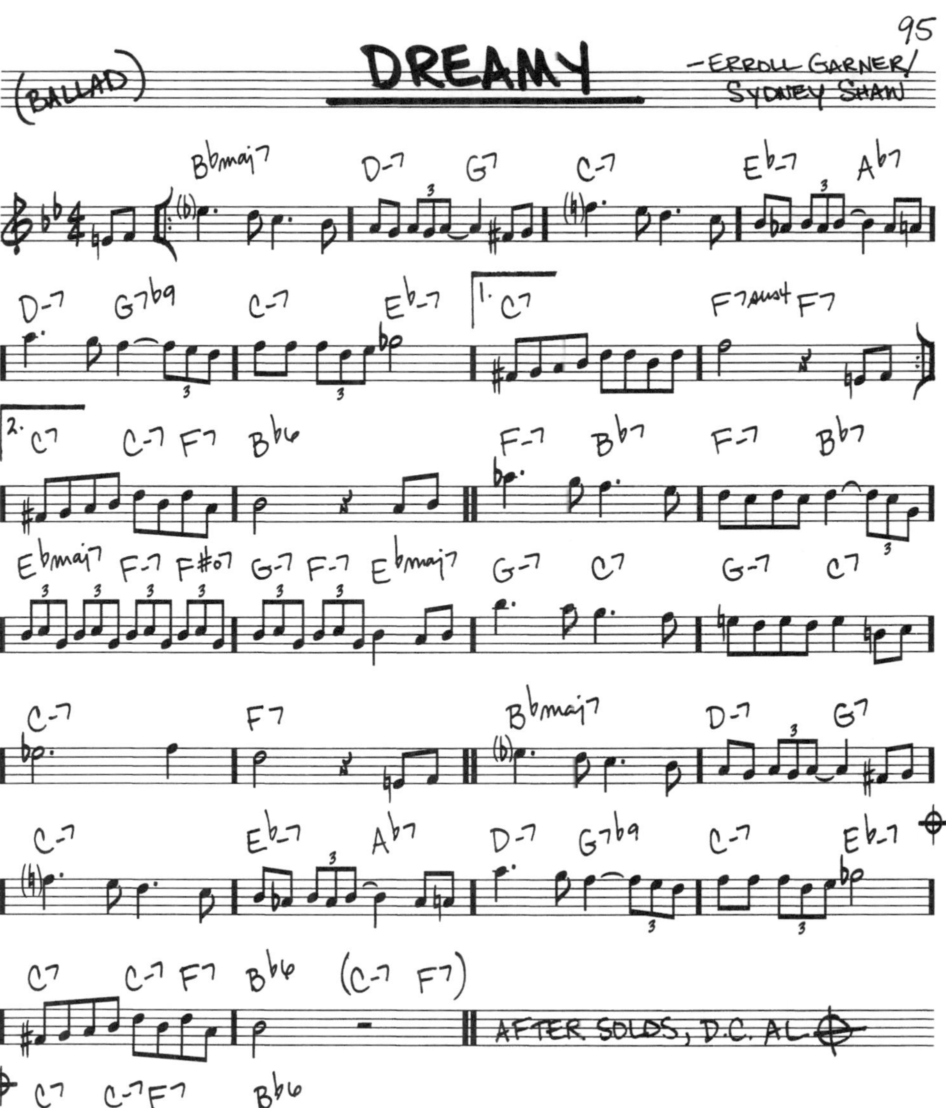
(BALLAD)
DREAMY
—ERROLL GARNER/
SYDNEY SHAW
Bbmaj7 D-7 G7 C-7 Eb-7 Ab7
D-7 G7b9 C-7 Eb-7 1. C7 F7sus4 F7
2. C7 C-7 F7 Bb6 F-7 Bb7 F-7 Bb7
Ebmaj7 F-7 F#o7 G-7 F-7 Ebmaj7 G-7 C7 G-7 C7
C-7 F7 Bbmaj7 D-7 G7
C-7 Eb-7 Ab7 D-7 G7b9 C-7 Eb-7
C7 C-7 F7 Bb6 (C-7 F7)
AFTER SOLOS, D.C. AL
C7 C-7 F7 Bb6
RIT.

(MED. UP)

THE DRIVE

- OLIVER E. NELSON

DUFF

—HAMPTON HAWES

(MED. BLUES)
EARLY MORNING MOOD
-CHET BAKER
G6
C7
C#o7
G6
G7
G7#5
C7
G6
B-7
Bb-7
A-7
D7
3
G6
C7
G6
(D7)

ECLYPSO

—TOMMY FLANAGAN

(MED.)

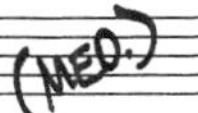

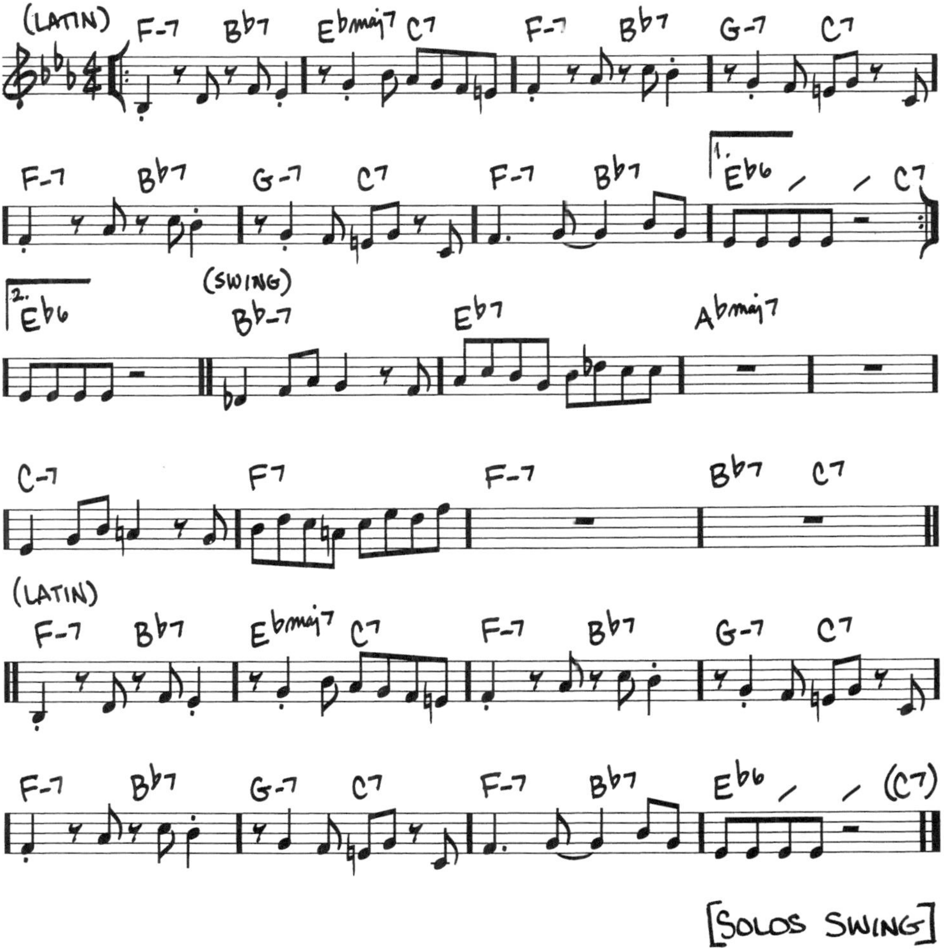
(LATIN)
F-7 Bb7 Ebmaj7 C7 F-7 Bb7 G-7 C7
F-7 Bb7 G-7 C7 F-7 Bb7
1.
Eb6 C7
2.
Eb6
(SWING)
Bb-7 Eb7 Abmaj7
C-7 F7 F-7 Bb7 C7
(LATIN)
F-7 Bb7 Ebmaj7 C7 F-7 Bb7 G-7 C7
F-7 Bb7 G-7 C7 F-7 Bb7 Eb6 (C7)
[SOLOS SWING]

East to Wes

— Emily Remler

(Bossa)

G- F7 E♭maj7 D-7 G- G-(add9) G-

G- F7 E♭maj7 D-7 A7♯5 D7♯9

G7♯9 C13 F13♯9 B♭13 E♭13♯9 D7♯5(♯9) G-

G7♯9 C13 F13♯9 B♭13 E♭13♯9 D7♭5(♭9)

G- F7 E♭maj7 D-7 G- G-(add9) G-

C-7 F7 B♭maj7 E♭maj7 A-7♭5 D7

G7(♯9) C7 F7 B♭maj7 A-7♭5 D7 ⊕ D♭9(♯11) C7

Bmaj7 B♭maj7 A-7♭5 D7 (To Solos)

SOLOS
Ebmaj7 A-7b5 D7b9 Ebmaj7 A-7b5 D7b9
(PLAY 4x)
G-7 A-7b5 D7b9 G-7 G7
C-7 F7 Bbmaj7 Ebmaj7
A-7b5 D7b9 G-7 Bb7 A-7b5 D7b9
G-7 A-7b5 D7b9 G-7 G7
C-7 F7 Bbmaj7 Ebmaj7
A-7b5 D7b9 G-7 F-7 Bb7
Ebmaj7 A-7b5 D7b9 Ebmaj7 A-7b5 D7b9
(PLAY 4x)
AFTER SOLOS, D.C. AL ⊕
⊕
Db9(#11) C7 Bmaj7 Bbmaj7 A-7b5 D7
[OPT. ENDING]
G-
REPEAT AND FADE

ELOGIE
(MED. UP ♩=118)
- EARL BUD POWELL
TWO-BEAT FEEL
C-11
Eb-11
Dbmaj7
Db7/Ab
Gb9
B13
F7sus4
Ab7sus4
Dbmaj7
Db7/Ab
Gb9
B13
Ab7sus4
Ab7
Dbmaj7
FINE
SOLO Db RHYTHM CHANGES
BASS WALKS ON SOLOS

ELORA

-J.J. JOHNSON

104
(MED. BLUES)
EMANCIPATION BLUES
-OLIVER NELSON
INTRO
G7 C6 G7
C6 G7
C6 G7
C6 G7
HEAD
G7
C7
G7
D7
C7
D7
C7
D7
C7
G7
1.
2.
AFTER SOLOS, D.S. AL ⊕
(PLAY PICKUPS)
G7 G13#11

ESTATE
(MED. BOSSA)
-BRUNO MARTINO/
BRUNO BRIGHETTI
D-7 G-7 A7 D-7 G-7 C7
Fmaj7 Bbmaj7 G-7 E-7 A7 Eb9
D-7 G-7 A7 D-7 G-7 C7
Fmaj7 Bbmaj7 G-7 E-7 A7 A7#5
Dmaj7 E-7 A7 Dmaj7 G-7 C7
Fmaj7 Bbmaj7 G-7 E-7 A7 Eb9
D-7 G-7 A7 D-7 G-7 C7
Fmaj7 Bbmaj7 G-7 E-7 A7 Eb9
D-7 G-7 A7#9 D-7 Bbmaj7 G-7 Eb9
AFTER SOLOS D.C. AL
G-7 A7#9 D-7

EYE OF THE HURRICANE
(MED. UP SWING)
-HERBIE HANCOCK
F-6 Bb6 Eb7sus4 Ab7sus4 Dbmaj7 C7#9 N.C. Gb-7 Bb-7
N.C. Eb7#9/F
N.C. F-7
F-6 Bb6 Eb7sus4 Ab7sus4 Dbmaj7 C7#9 N.C. Gb-7 Bb-7
N.C. Eb7#9/F
N.C. F-7
3 3 3 3
3 3 3 3
[SOLOS ON F- BLUES]

♩=69 (EVEN 8THS)
FARMER'S TRUST
—PAT METHENY
A
G B-7 G/B C#-7 F#7b9 F#7b9/B B-
A-7 D7sus4 D7 F/G G F/G Cadd9 Gsus4 G G7
Csus4 C E-7 C/E Ab Bb Db/Eb Eb Db/Eb
Abadd9 G7#5(#9) Gb6/9 G-7b5/Db C7b9
B
F-9 C-9 G-11 Abmaj7 Ab7
1. Csus4 C Abmaj7 Bb/Ab Csus4 C D
2. Csus4 C Abmaj7 Bb/Ab Csus4 C D
AFTER SOLOS, D.C. AL ⊕
⊕ Csus4 C Abmaj7 Bb/Ab Csus4 C 1. 2.

(MED. ROCK)
FEELS SO GOOD
—CHUCK MANGIONE
C9sus4
F
C/E
D-7
G-7
C
C/Bb
A-7
D-7
G-7
E-7b5
A7#5
D-7
Ebmaj9
D-7
Ebmaj9
F
Ebadd9
D-
D/C
Bbmaj7
F/A
G-7
G-
A-
Bb
Bo7
C7sus4
N.C.
F
D7
(D7)
G-7
C7sus4
F
D7

(D7)
G-7
C9sus4
(ENDING)
Fmaj7
D.S. FOR SOLOS

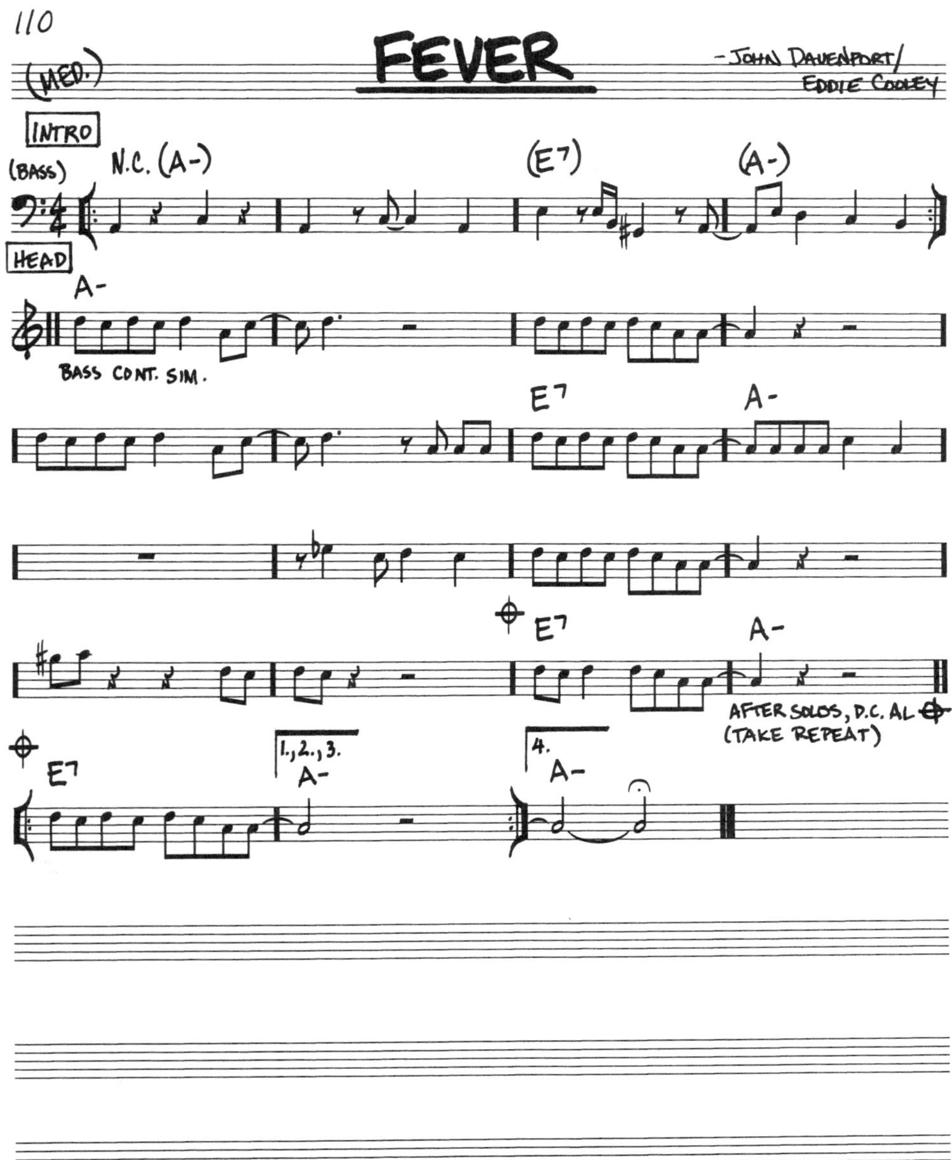
FEVER
(MED.)
- JOHN DAVENPORT/
EDDIE COOLEY
INTRO
(BASS)
N.C. (A-)
(E7)
(A-)
HEAD
A-
BASS CONT. SIM.
E7
A-
E7
A-
AFTER SOLOS, D.C. AL
(TAKE REPEAT)
E7
1., 2., 3.
A-
4.
A-

FIELDS OF GOLD
MED. (EVEN 8THS)
— STING

52nd STREET THEME

(UP)

–THELONIOUS MONK

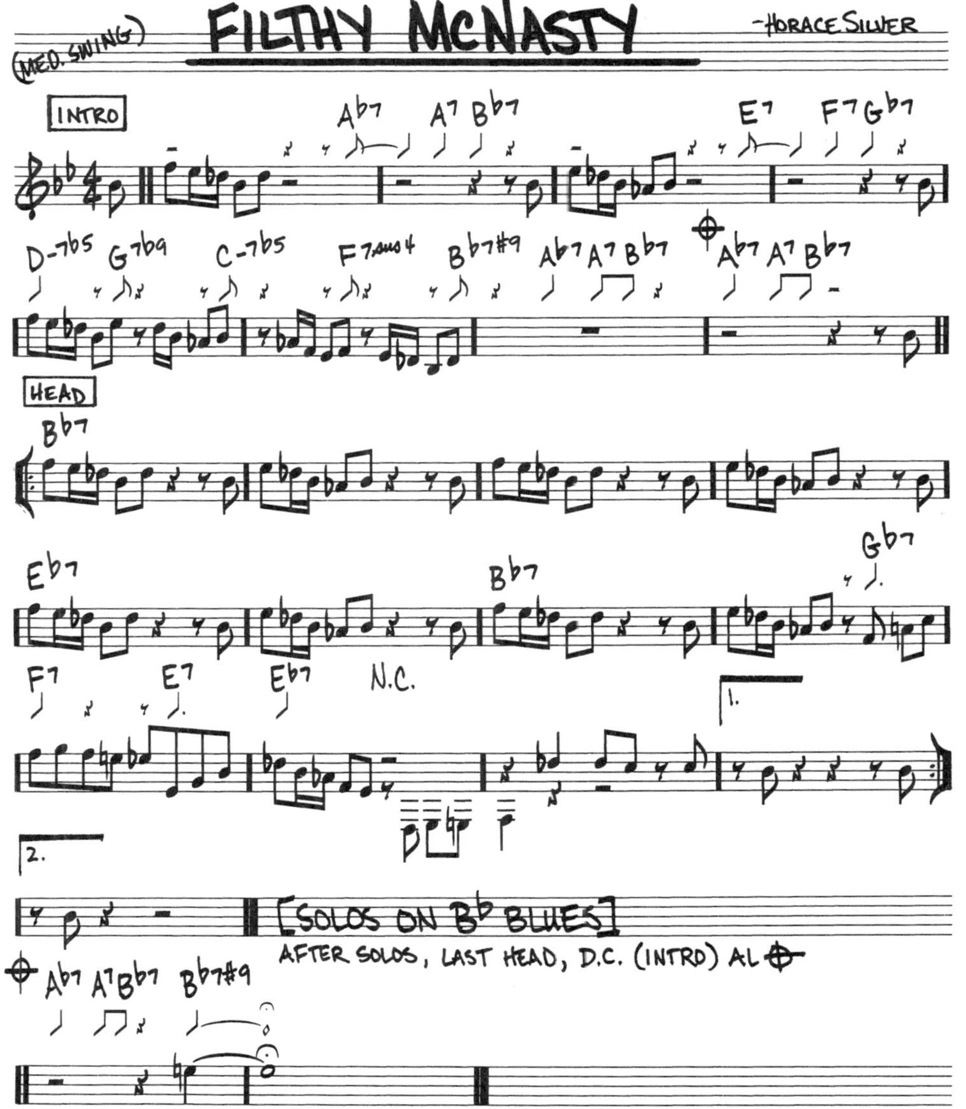
(MED. SWING)
FILTHY McNASTY
-HORACE SILVER
INTRO
Ab7 A7 Bb7
E7 F7 Gb7
D-7b5 G7b9 C-7b5 F7sus4 Bb7#9 Ab7 A7 Bb7
Ab7 A7 Bb7
HEAD
Bb7
Eb7
Bb7
Gb7
F7 E7 Eb7 N.C.
1.
2.
[SOLOS ON Bb BLUES]
AFTER SOLOS, LAST HEAD, D.C. (INTRO) AL
Ab7 A7 Bb7 Bb7#9

FIVE BROTHERS

–GERRY MULLIGAN

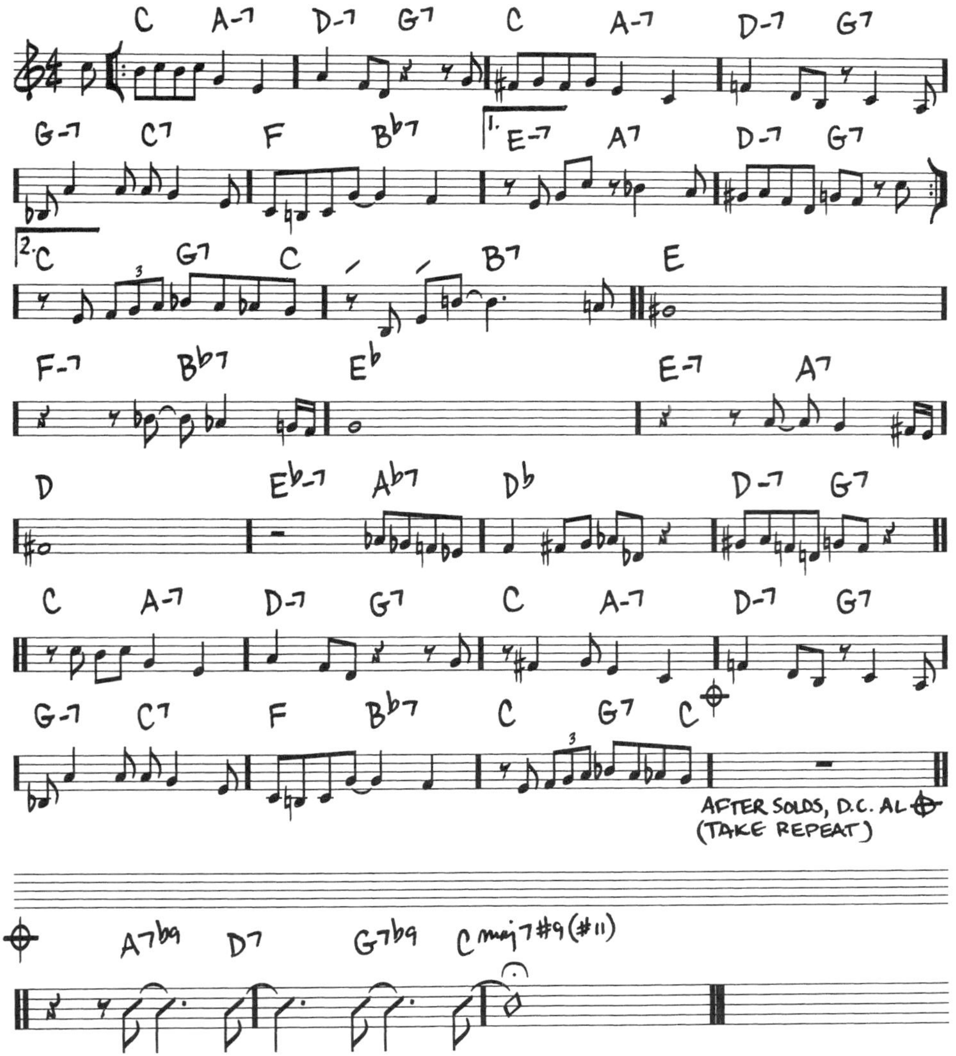

C A–7 D–7 G7 C A–7 D–7 G7

G–7 C7 F B♭7 1. E–7 A7 D–7 G7

2. C G7 C B7 E

F–7 B♭7 E♭ E–7 A7

D E♭–7 A♭7 D♭ D–7 G7

C A–7 D–7 G7 C A–7 D–7 G7

G–7 C7 F B♭7 C G7 C ⊕

AFTER SOLOS, D.C. AL ⊕
(TAKE REPEAT)

⊕ A7♭9 D7 G7♭9 Cmaj7♯9(♯11)

A FLOWER IS A LOVESOME THING

(BALLAD)

— BILLY STRAYHORN

FLY ME TO THE MOON
(IN OTHER WORDS)

(MED. SWING) — BART HOWARD

FLYING HOME

(MED. SWING)

– BENNY GOODMAN/
LIONEL HAMPTON

E♭ E♭/D♭ C-7 B7 B♭7 E♭ E♭/D♭ C-7 B7 B♭7

E♭ E♭/D♭ C-7 B7 B♭7 E♭6 1. B♭7 2. (E♭6)

E♭7 A♭7

(BALLAD)

THE FOLKS WHO LIVE ON THE HILL

- JEROME KERN/OSCAR HAMMERSTEIN

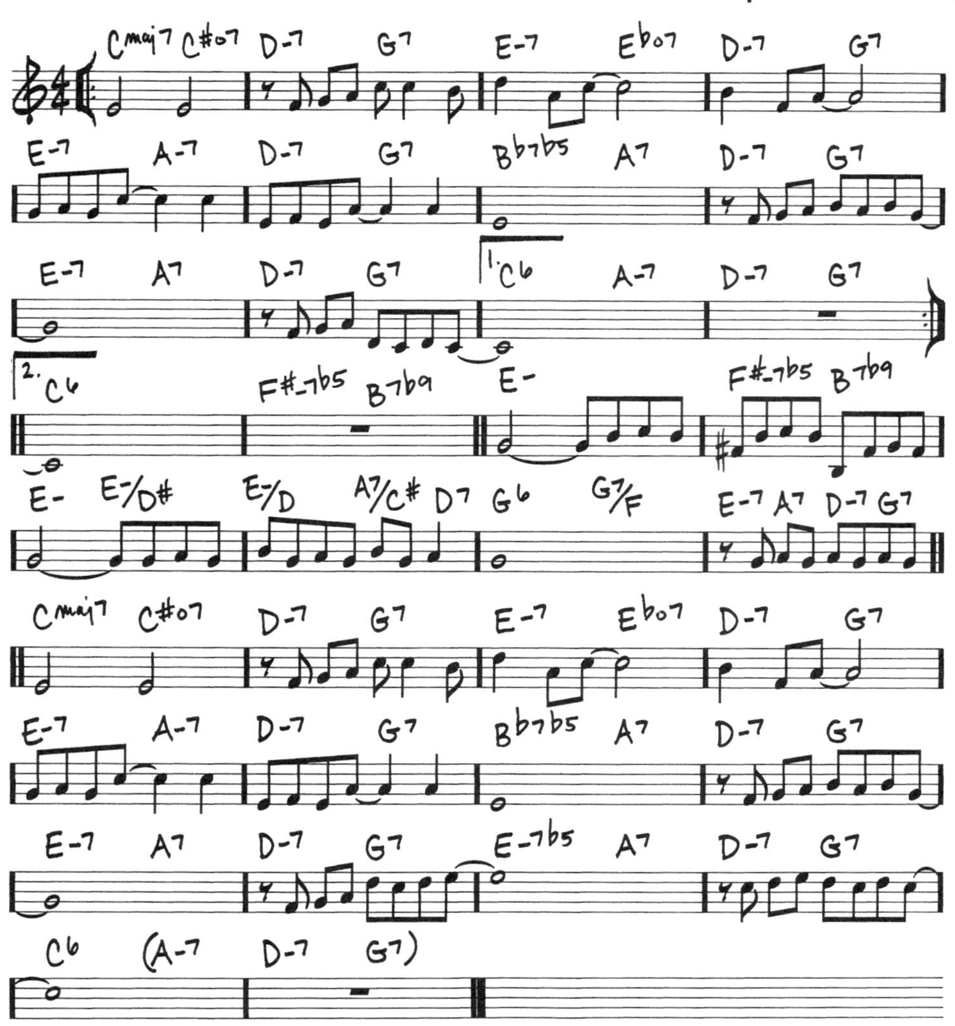

FREIGHT TRANE

(MED. UP)

—TOMMY FLANAGAN

FOX HUNT

(UP)

-J.J. JOHNSON

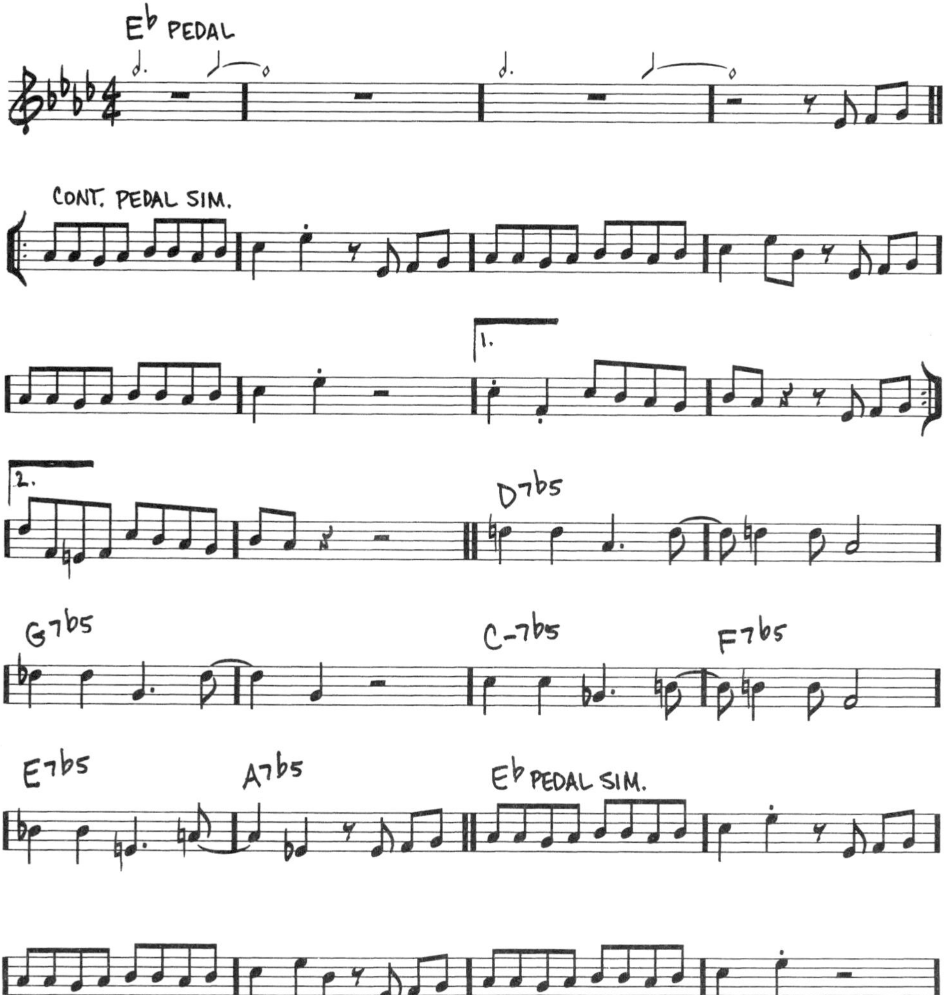

E♭ PEDAL

CONT. PEDAL SIM.

1.

2.

D7♭5

G7♭5

C-7♭5

F7♭5

E7♭5

A7♭5

E♭ PEDAL SIM.

FINE
(TO SOLOS)
SOLOS RHYTHM CHANGES
Ab A°7 Bb-7 Eb7 Ab A°7 Bb-7 Eb7 Ab Ab7 Db D°7 Ab Eb7 Ab
D7b5 G7b5 C-7b5 F7b5 E7b5 A7b5
Ab A°7 Bb-7 Eb7 Ab A°7 Bb-7 Eb7 Ab Ab7 Db D°7 Ab Eb7 Ab
AFTER SOLOS, D.C. AL FINE

FRENESÍ

(BOSSA)

– ALBERTO DOMINGUEZ

(EASY SWING)

THE FRIM FRAM SAUCE

– JOE RICARDEL/
REDD EVANS

(MED.)
FULL MOON AND EMPTY ARMS
-BUDDY KAYE / TED MOSSMAN
Bbmaj7
Ab-7
Db7
Bbmaj7
C-7b5
F7
Bbmaj7
D7
G-7
C-7
F7
1. Bbmaj7
G-7
C7
C-7
F7
2. Bbmaj7
Ab7
G7
C-7
F7b9
Bb6
(C-7
F7)

(MED. UP SWING)

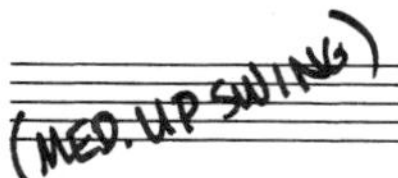

FUNKALLERO

- BILL EVANS

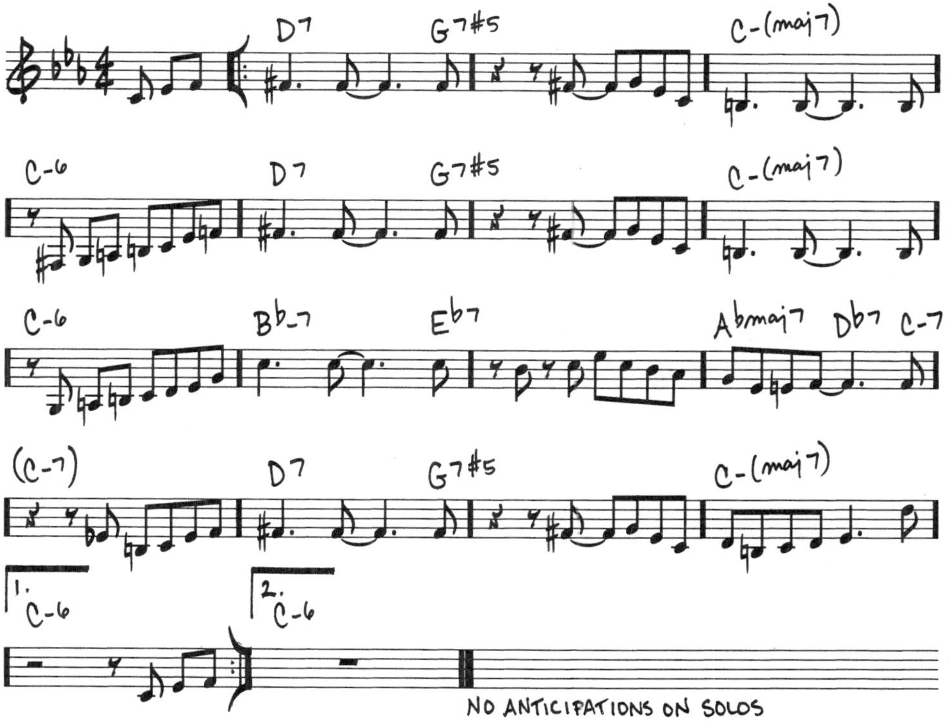
D7
G7#5
C-(maj7)
C-6
D7
G7#5
C-(maj7)
C-6
Bb-7
Eb7
Abmaj7
Db7
C-7
(C-7)
D7
G7#5
C-(maj7)
1. C-6
2. C-6

NO ANTICIPATIONS ON SOLOS

FUNKY

— KENNY BURRELL

(MED. BLUES)

(BALLAD)

GEORGIA ON MY MIND

– HOAGY CARMICHAEL / STUART GORRELL

GETTIN' IT TOGETHA
(MED. FAST EVEN 8ths)
- BOBBY TIMMONS
G-7
C-7
8vb
G-7
C-7
8vb
N.C.
D7#5
G-7
C
G-7
C
G-7
C-7
C-7/Bb
A-7b5
Abmaj7
D-7b5
G7#5
C-7
D7#5
G-7
C
G-7
C
G-7
C-7
C-7/Bb
A-7b5
Abmaj7
D-7b5
G7#5
C-7
(D7#5)
FINE
SOLOS
G-7
4
C-7
4
AFTER SOLOS, D.C. AL FINE

THE GIFT!
(RECADO BOSSA NOVA)

-DJALMA FERREIRA/
LUIZ ANTONIO/
PAUL FRANCIS WEBSTER

(BOSSA)

D-7 A7
D7 G-7 G-7/F
E-7b5 A7b9 D-7 1. D-7/C
B-7b5 E7b9 E-7b5 A7b9
2. (D-7) C-7 A7b9 D-7
D7b9 G-7
E7b9 A-7 A7b9
D-7 A7
D7 G-7
E-7b5 A7b9 D-7
C-7 A7b9 D-7 (E-7b5 A7b9)

FINE

(SLOW SWING)

GIRL TALK

– NEAL HEFTI/
BOBBY TROUP

(BALLAD)
GLAD TO BE UNHAPPY
- RICHARD RODGERS / LORENZ HART
G-7 Eb7 G-7 C7 G-7 C7
G-7 Eb7 G-7 C7 F F7#5
Bbmaj7 C7 A-7 D7 G-7 C7 F F7#5
Bbmaj7 B-7 E7 A-7 D7b9 G-7 C7 F D7#5(#9)
G-7 Eb7 G-7 C7 G-7 C7
A-7b5 D7 G-7 C7b9 F6 (A-7 D7b9)

THE GLORY OF LOVE

(MED.)

- BILLY HILL

GREGORY IS HERE

- HORACE SILVER

(MED. LATIN)

𝄋 A

*B13(#11) C-11

*C#/B

B13(#11) C-11

A-7b5 D7b9 G-7 C7

C-9 B7#9 Bbmaj7 ⊕ 1. 2.

B

Eb-7 Ab7 Dbmaj7 Bb-7

Eb-7 Ab7 C-11 F7 N.C.

D.S. AL ⊕

⊕

SOLO A A B A

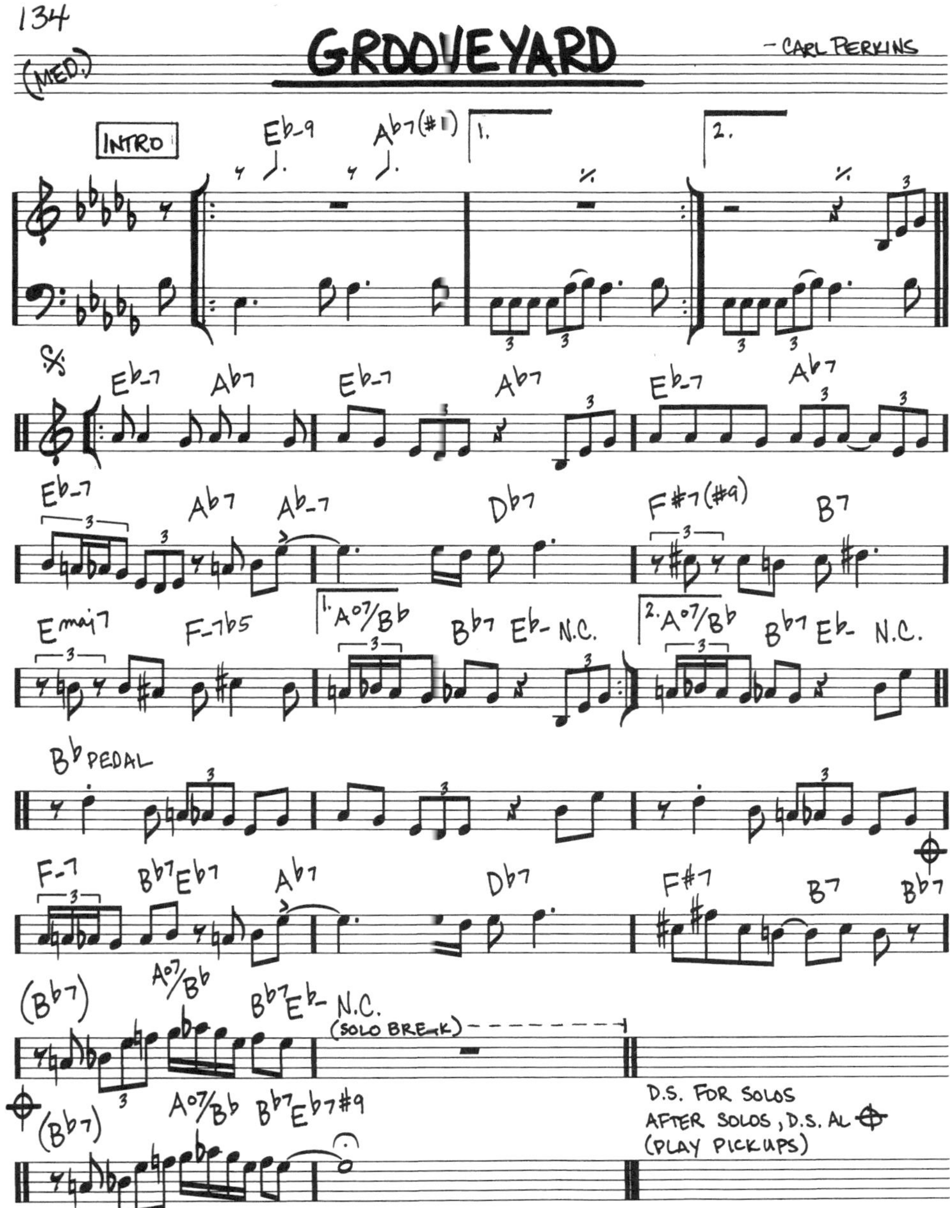
134
GROOVEYARD
– CARL PERKINS
(MED.)
INTRO
Eb-9 Ab7(#11)
1.
2.
Eb-7 Ab7 Eb-7 Ab7 Eb-7 Ab7
Eb-7 Ab7 Ab-7 Db7 F#7(#9) B7
Emaj7 F-7b5 1. A°7/Bb Bb7 Eb- N.C. 2. A°7/Bb Bb7 Eb- N.C.
Bb PEDAL
F-7 Bb7 Eb7 Ab7 Db7 F#7 B7 Bb7
(Bb7) A°7/Bb Bb7 Eb- N.C.
(SOLO BREAK)
(Bb7) A°7/Bb Bb7 Eb7#9
D.S. FOR SOLOS
AFTER SOLOS, D.S. AL ⊕
(PLAY PICKUPS)

H & H

—PAT METHENY

HACKENSACK

(MED. UP SWING)

—THELONIOUS MONK

(FAST BOP)

HALLUCINATIONS

—EARL "BUD" POWELL

(UP)

HAPPY LITTLE SUNBEAM

– RUSSELL FREEMAN

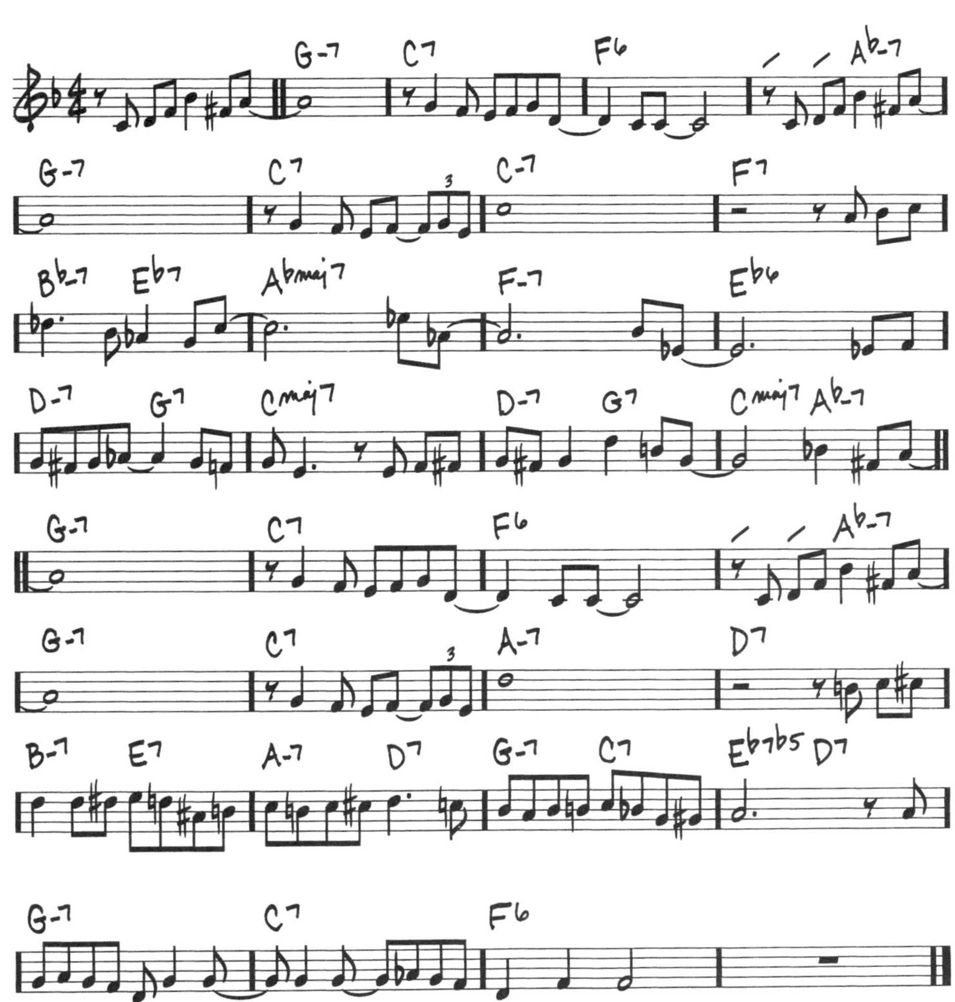

(MED. SWING)

HARLEM NOCTURNE

– EARLE HAGEN/
DICK ROGERS

(Easy Swing)

Hard Hearted Hanna
(The Vamp of Savannah)

— Jack Yellen / Milton Ager / Bob Bigelow / Charles Bates

F7
Bb7
A7
Bb7
Eb6
C-7
B7
Bb7
Eb6
D7
Db7
C7
F-
G7
C-
B7
Bb-7
A7b5
Ab6
B7
Eb6
Db7
C7
F7
F-7
Bb7
Eb6
Bb7
SOLOS OVER B
AFTER SOLOS, D.S. AL
Eb6

HAVONA

-JACO PASTORIUS

Bmaj7(#11)
Gmaj7
Asus4 Bsus4
Asus4 Bsus4
Asus4 Bsus4
N.C.
(UNISON)
SOLO ON A
AFTER SOLOS, PLAY A TWICE
TAKE ⊕ 2nd TIME
Asus4 Bsus4
REPEAT AS DESIRED
ON CUE:
Dsus4
Csus4 Bsus4 Asus4 G#sus4 F#sus4 Bsus4 G#sus4 F#sus4 Bsus4 Esus4
F#sus4 G#sus4 Esus4

144
(MED. FAST)
HEAD AND SHOULDERS
-CEDAR WALTON
Ab7 G7 Gb7 F7 Ab7 G7
Gb7 F7 Emaj7b5 Eb-7 Dmaj7b5
Db-7 Gb7 Cbmaj7
C-7b5 F7 1. Bb-7 Eb7 2. Bb-7 Eb7
Dmaj7 Cmaj7 Dmaj7 Eb7 Fmaj7 Ebmaj7
Fmaj7 F#7 / / Dmaj9 Ab7#5/C Db6/9
3

HIGH FLY

(MED. SWING)

— RANDY WESTON

HI BECK
(MED. UP)
– LEE KONITZ
Cmaj7 C#o7 Dmaj7 Db7
Cmaj7 Dmaj7 Dbmaj7
C7 F6
D7 G7
Cmaj7 C#o7 Dmaj7 Dbmaj7
G-7b5 C7 Fmaj7
Fmaj7 Bb7 Ebmaj7 Dbmaj7
D-7 G7 Cmaj7 (D-7 G7)

SOLOS

Cmaj7 | E-7 Eb°7 | D-7 | G7 | Cmaj7 | E-7 Eb°7 | D-7 | G7
C7 | | Fmaj7 | | D7 | | D-7 | G7
Cmaj7 | E-7 Eb°7 | D-7 | G7 | G-7 | C7 | Fmaj7 |
Fmaj7 | Bb7 | E-7 | A7 | D-7 | G7 | Cmaj7 | D-7 G7

HIT THAT MESS
(MED.)
– HARRY D. SQUIRES/BULEE GAILLARD
F7
Bb7
F6
G-7
C7
F6
Bb7
F6
C7
F7
Bb7
F6
G-7
C7
F6
Bb7
F6
(C7)

(BOSSA)
HO-BA-LA-LA
-NORMAN GIMBEL/
JOAO GILBERTO
A-7
F#-7b5
B7
E-7
A7b9
A-7
D7
1. G6
B-7b5
E7
2. G6
Db7b5
C-7
F7
Bbmaj7
Bo7
C-7
F7
A-7
D7
B-7b5
E7
A-7
F#-7b5
B7
E-7
A7b9
A-7
D7
G6
(B-7b5
E7)

HOLY LAND

(MED.)

— CEDAR WALTON

(MED.)

HONEYSUCKLE ROSE

—THOMAS "FATS" WALLER/
ANDY RAZAF

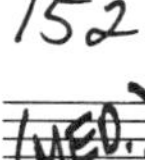

HORACE SCOPE

– HORACE SILVER

(MED.)

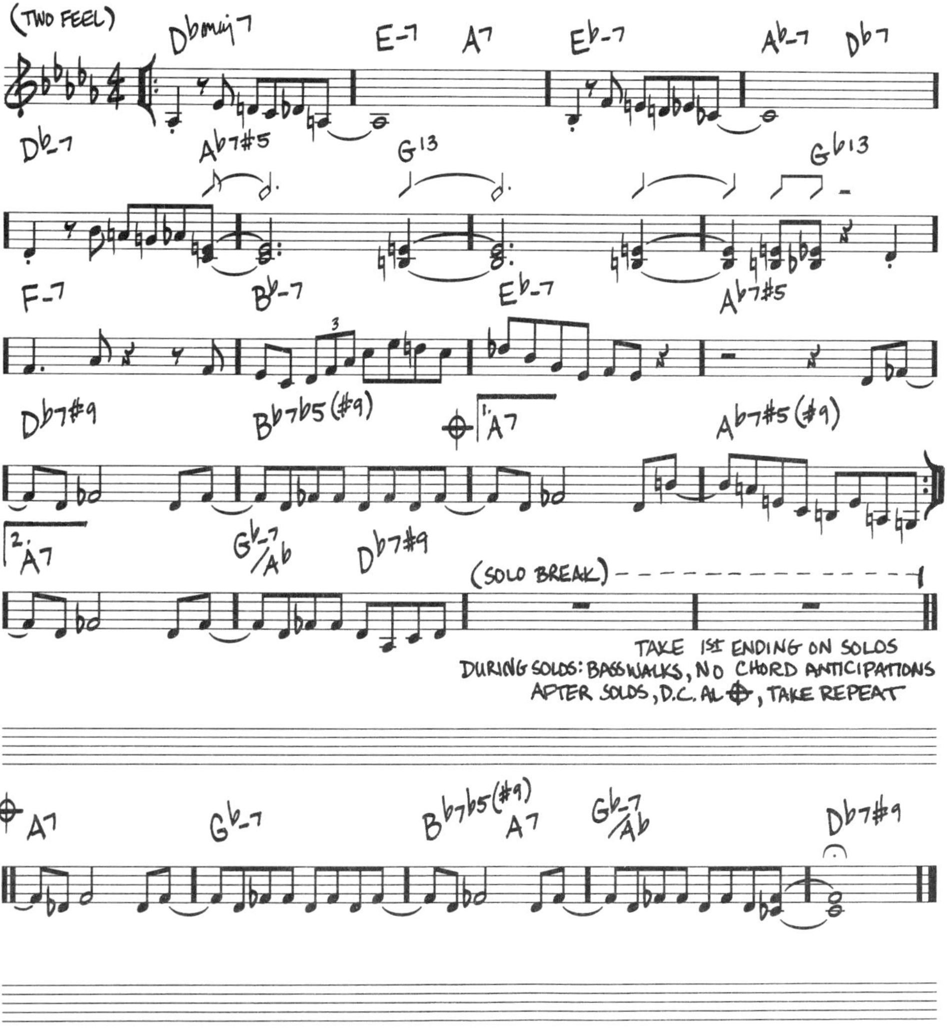
(TWO FEEL)
Dbmaj7
E-7
A7
Eb-7
Ab-7
Db7
Db-7
Ab7#5
G13
Gb13
F-7
Bb-7
3
Eb-7
Ab7#5
Db7#9
Bb7b5(#9)
1. A7
Ab7#5(#9)
2. A7
Gb-7/Ab
Db7#9
(SOLO BREAK)
TAKE 1st ENDING ON SOLOS
DURING SOLOS: BASS WALKS, NO CHORD ANTICIPATIONS
AFTER SOLOS, D.C. AL ⊕, TAKE REPEAT
A7
Gb-7
Bb7b5(#9)
A7
Gb-7/Ab
Db7#9

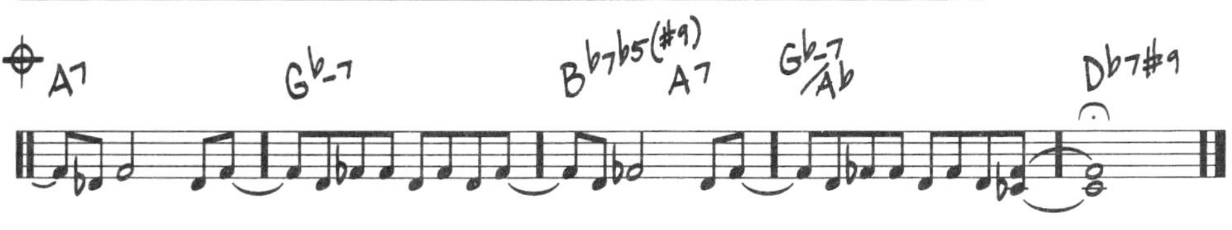

(BALLAD) HOW ARE THINGS IN GLOCCA MORRA

-BURTON LANE/E.Y. HARBURG

THE HUCKLEBUCK

(MED. SWING)

-ANDY GIBSON

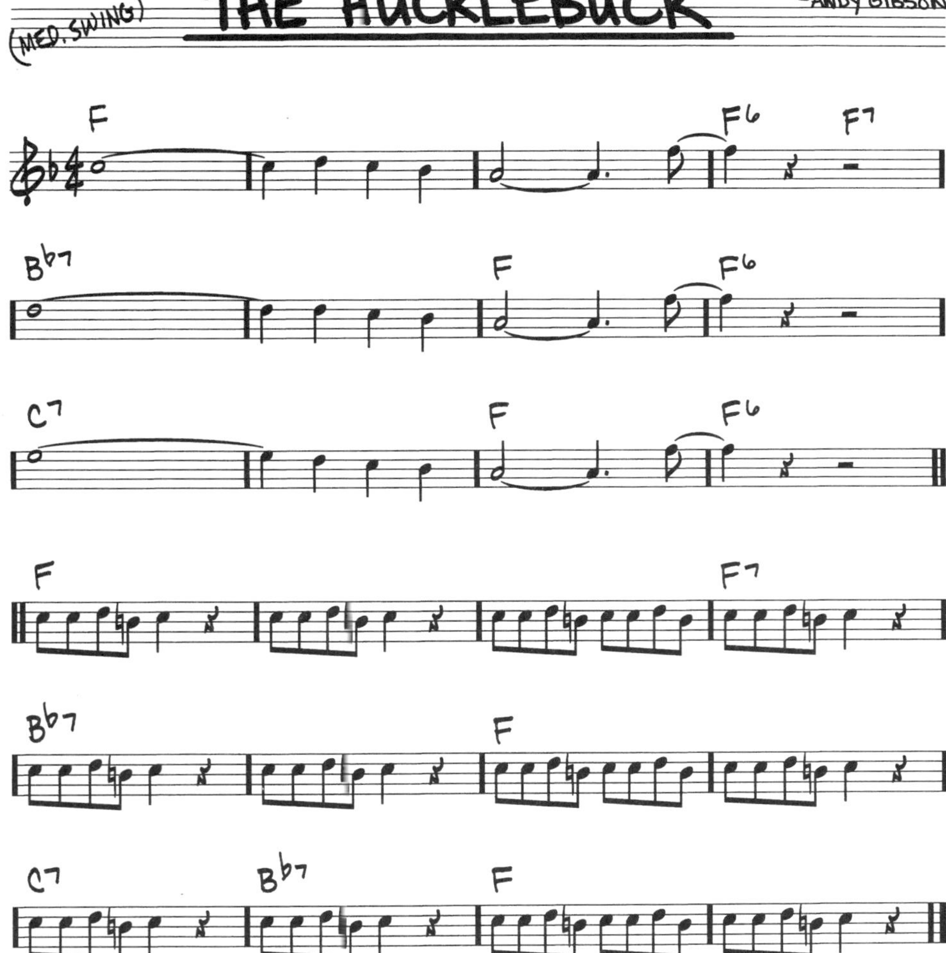

HUMPTY DUMPTY
- CHICK COREA
(FAST SWING)
Ebmaj7
Dmaj7
Gbmaj7
Fmaj7
A7#5
Bbmaj7
Bb-7
(Bb-7)
N.C.
D-7
B-7
Ab-7
F-7
Ab-7
Gbmaj7
Bb-7
NO ANTICIPATIONS ON SOLOS
AFTER SOLOS, D.C. AL
Gbmaj7
Emaj7
D7
Db-7
Gb7
Bmaj7
Bb7
Eb-7
C-7
A-7

156
I BELIEVE IN YOU
- FRANK LOESSER
(MED. UP)
A
A- A-(maj7) A-7
A-6 B-7 C9#11 B-7 E7
A- A-(maj7) A-7 A-6
Bmaj7 C#-7 F#7 Bmaj7 A-7 D7
Gmaj7 B-7 E7 A-7 D7
1. G6 E7
2. G6 Bb-7 Eb7
B
Abmaj7 Bb-7 Eb7 Abmaj7 C-7 F7
Bb-7 Eb7 Abmaj7 C-7 F7
Bbmaj7 C-7 F7 Bbmaj7
G-7 C7 A-7 D7 B-7 E7
D.S. AL
G6 (B-7 E7)
(LAST x)
SOLO ON ENTIRE FORM A A B A
© 1961 (Renewed) FRANK MUSIC CORP.

(MED.) I CAN'T BELIEVE THAT YOU'RE IN LOVE WITH ME

-JIMMY MCHUGH/CLARENCE GASKILL

F6 B♭7 Cmaj7 D7

G7 Cmaj7 G-7 C7

F6 B♭7 Cmaj7 D7

G7 C6 F7 C6

E7 A7

D7 G7 C7

F6 B♭7 Cmaj7 D7

G7 C6 (G-7 C7)

(MED.) I DIDN'T KNOW WHAT TIME IT WAS

-RICHARD RODGERS/LORENZ HART

(BALLAD) I GOTTA RIGHT TO SING THE BLUES

-HAROLD ARLEN/TED KOEHLER

(MED. OR BALLAD)
I GET ALONG WITHOUT YOU VERY WELL
(EXCEPT SOMETIMES)
— HOAGY CARMICHAEL
Bbmaj7 G-7 C-7 F7 Bbmaj7 Ebmaj7 D-7 Db°7
C-7 F7 C-7 F7
C-7 B7#5 C-7 F7
1. Bbmaj7 Ebmaj7 D-7 Db°7 C-7 F7
C-7 G7#5 C-7 F7 Bbmaj7 B°7 C-7 F7
2. Bb6 Ebmaj7 D-7 Db°7 C-7 F7
Bbmaj7 D-7 Db°7 C-7 F7
Bbmaj7 F7 Bbmaj7 Eb6 Eb/D C-7 F7

B♭maj7 E♭7
D7 A♭7
G-7
C7
C-7
F7
B♭maj7 G-7
C-7 F7
B♭maj7 E♭maj7
D-7 D♭o7
C-7
F7
C-7
F7
C-7
B7♯5
C-7
F7
B♭6 (D♭o7
C-7 F7)

(BALLAD)

I HAVE DREAMED

– RICHARD RODGERS/
OSCAR HAMMERSTEIN II

(MED. SWING)

I HEAR A RHAPSODY

-GEORGE FRAGOS/
JACK BAKER/
DICK GASPARRE

(BALLAD)

I LEFT MY HEART IN SAN FRANCISCO

-GEORGE CORY/DOUGLASS CROSS

(MED.)
I LIKE THE LIKES OF YOU
- VERNON DUKE/E.Y. HARBURG

I REMEMBER BIRD
(BLUESY BALLAD)
-LEONARD FEATHER
F-7 B♭7
E♭-7 A♭7
C-7 F7
B♭7
C7
F7
F-7 B♭7
E♭-7 A♭7
C-7 F7
B♭7
C7
F7
A♭7 G7
G-7
C7
F7 (B♭7 B°7 F7/C D♭7 C7)
SOLOS
F7
B♭7
F7
B♭7
A7
A♭7
G7
G-7
B♭-7
E♭7
A-7
D7
G-7
C7

(MED.)

I REMEMBER YOU

–VICTOR SCHERTZINGER/
JOHNNY MERCER

(MED. OR BALLAD)

I WILL WAIT FOR YOU

- MICHEL LEGRAND/
JACQUES DEMY/
NORMAN GIMBEL

(BALLAD) I WISH I DIDN'T LOVE YOU SO

– FRANK LOESSER

E♭6 C-7 G-7 F-7 B♭7 E♭maj7 B♭-7 E♭7 A♭maj7 A♭-7 D♭7

E♭maj7 C-7 F-7 B♭7 1. E♭6 C-7 F-7 B♭7

2. E♭6 A♭-6 E♭6 G-7♭5 C7

F-7 D♭7 C7

C-7 F7 F-7 B♭7 E♭6 C-7 G-7 F-7 B♭7

E♭maj7 B♭-7 E♭7 A♭maj7 A♭-7 D♭7 E♭maj7 C-7 F-7 B♭7

E♭6 (C-7 F-7 B♭7)

(MED.)
I WISH I WERE IN LOVE AGAIN
-RICHARD RODGERS/LORENZ HART
Gmaj7 C9#11 Gmaj7 C9#11
Gmaj7 C9#11 1. B-7 B♭o7 A-7 D7
2. A-7 D7 Gmaj7 G7 Cmaj7 F7 G6 E7
A-7 D7 G6 G7 Cmaj7 F7 G6 E7#5
A7 D7 Gmaj7 C9#11
Gmaj7 C9#11 Gmaj7 B-7 E-7
A-7 D7 G6 (A-7 D7)

BALLAD (OR MED. SWING)
I WISH YOU LOVE
– CHARLES TRENET/ ALBERT BEACH
C7b9 F-7 Bb7 G-7
Gbo7 F-7 1. Bb7 Eb6 Abmaj7
G-7b5 C7b9 2. Bb7 Bb-7 Eb7
Abmaj7 Ab-7 Db7 Ebmaj7 Abmaj7 G-7b5 C7#5
F-7 C-7 F7 F-7 Bb7 G-7b5 C7b9
F-7 Bb7 G-7 Gbo7
F-7 Bb7 Eb6 (G-7b5 C7b9)

I'LL KNOW

(MED.)

—FRANK LOESSER

(MED. BALLAD)

I'M A FOOL TO WANT YOU

-JACK WOLF/JOEL HERRON/FRANK SINATRA

E-7 / / E7b9 A-7

F#-7b5 B7b9 E-7 1.A-7 C9

B7 B7b9 2.A-7 F#-7b5 B7b9 E-7

A- A-(maj7) A-7 D7 Gmaj7 G6

A- A-(maj7) A-7 D7 Gmaj7 G6

F#-7b5 B7b9 E-7

G-7 C9 F#-7b5 B7b9

E-7 / / E7b9 A-7 F#-7b5 B7b9

E-7 C9 A-7 F#-7b5 B7b9

E-7 (B7#5b9)

I'M JUST A LUCKY SO AND SO

(MED.)

-DUKE ELLINGTON/MACK DAVID

I'M SITTING ON TOP OF THE WORLD

(MED.)

—RAY HENDERSON/SAM M. LEWIS/JOE YOUNG

(MED.)

I'VE FOUND A NEW BABY
(I FOUND A NEW BABY)

—JACK PALMER/
SPENCER WILLIAMS

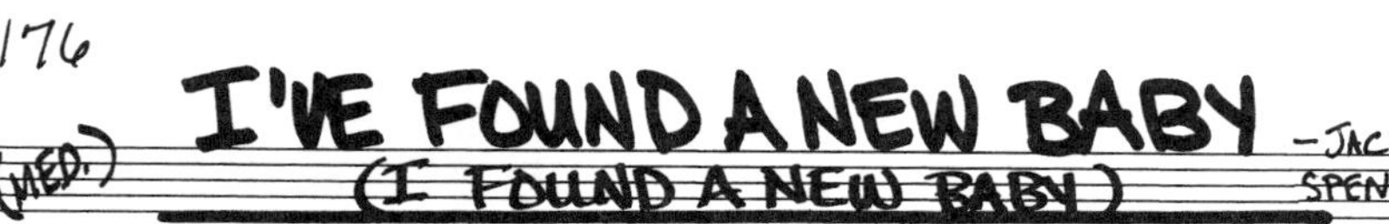

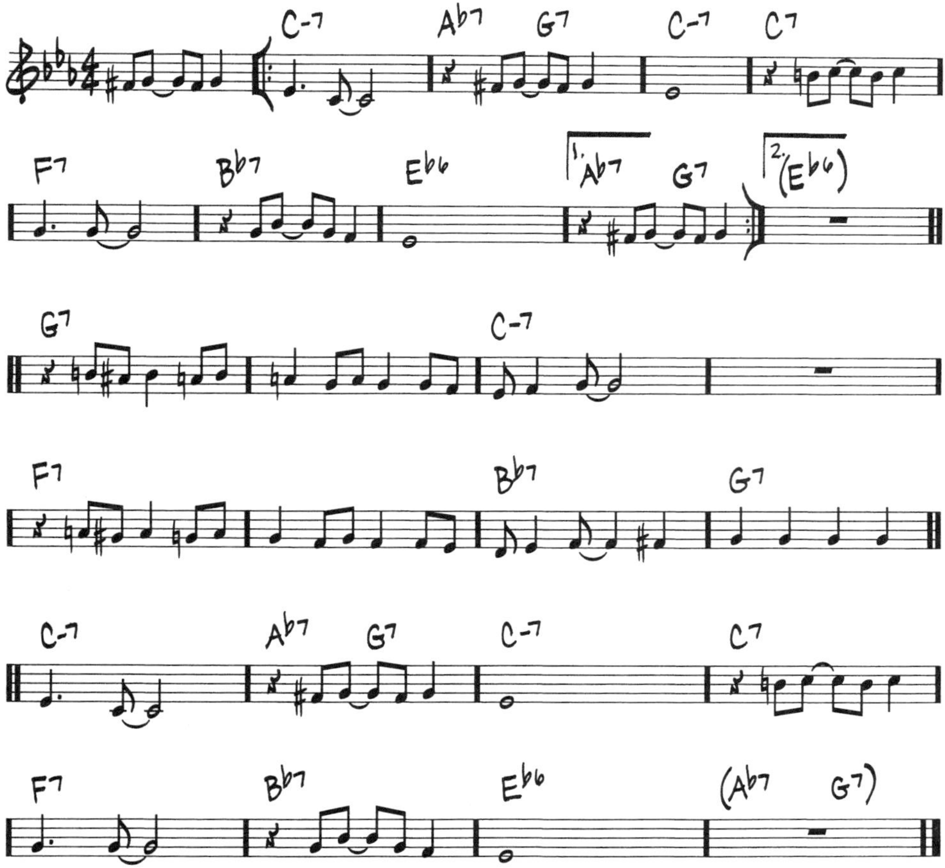
C-7
Ab7
G7
C-7
C7
F7
Bb7
Eb6
1. Ab7
G7
2. (Eb6)
G7
C-7
F7
Bb7
G7
C-7
Ab7
G7
C-7
C7
F7
Bb7
Eb6
(Ab7
G7)

(MED.)

I'VE TOLD EV'RY LITTLE STAR

—JEROME KERN/OSCAR HAMMERSTEIN II

F6 D-7 G-7 C7 A7b9 D-7 Bb-7 Eb7

A-7 D-7 G-7 C7 1. F6 D-7 G-7 C7 2. F6 D-7 G7

Cmaj7 D-7 G7 Cmaj7 C°7

B-7b5 E7b9 A-7 D-7 G7 G-7 C7

F6 D-7 G-7 C7 A7b9 D-7 Bb-7 Eb7

A-7 D-7 G-7 C7 F6 (G-7 C7)

(BRIGHT)

ICE CREAM KONITZ

—LEE KONITZ

IDOL GOSSIP
-GERRY MULLIGAN
(MED. UP)
D-7 Bb7#11
A7sus4/E A7#5 D-11 1. A7#9 2. C-7 F7
Bbmaj7 B°7 C-7 F7 Bbmaj7 B°7 C-7 F7
Bbmaj7 B°7 C-7 F7 Bbmaj7 A7b9
D-7 Bb7#11
A7sus4/E A7#5 D-11
A7#9 D-11 (SOLO BREAK)
SOLOS
D-7 Bb7 E-7b5 A7 D-7 1. A7 2. C-7 F7
Bbmaj7 B°7 C-7 F7 Bbmaj7 B°7 C-7 F7 Bbmaj7 B°7 C-7 F7 Bbmaj7 G-7 E-7b5 A7
D-7 Bb7 E-7b5 A7 D-7 A7

(BALLAD OR MED.)

IF I LOVED YOU

-RICHARD RODGERS/
OSCAR HAMMERSTEIN II

(MED.)

IF I SHOULD LOSE YOU

—LEO ROBIN/
RALPH RAINGER

(MED.)

IF I WERE A BELL

-FRANK LOESSER

IMAGINATION

(MED. BALLAD)

—JIMMY VAN HEUSEN / JOHNNY BURKE

IN A LITTLE SPANISH TOWN
('TWAS ON A NIGHT LIKE THIS)

(MED. SWING)

—MABEL WAYNE / SAM M. LEWIS / JOE YOUNG

(MED. UP)
IN CASE YOU HAVEN'T HEARD
- WOODY SHAW
Bbmaj13 Abmaj13 Bbmaj13 Abmaj13 Abmaj7 Gbmaj13
Abmaj13 Gbmaj13 Abmaj13 Gbmaj13 Abmaj13 Bbmaj13 Cmaj13
Dbmaj7#11 Bmaj7#11 F7#9 E7#9 Eb7#9
G-7 A-7 Ab-7 Bb-7 A-7 B-7 D7
*Bbmaj13 Abmaj13 Bbmaj13 Abmaj13 Abmaj7 Gbmaj13
*RHY. AS BEFORE
Abmaj13 Gbmaj13 Abmaj13 Gbmaj13 Abmaj13 Bbmaj13 Cmaj13
Gbmaj7#11 Eb-7 Gbmaj7#11 B-7
Gbmaj7#11 Emaj7#11 Dmaj7#11 B-7 E7
SOLOS
Bmaj7#11 Dmaj7#11 Fmaj7#11 Abmaj7#11
8 8 8 8

(FAST LATIN)
IN PURSUIT OF THE 27th MAN
-HORACE SILVER
INTRO
N.C. *(C7sus4b9)
* G-7b5/C
HEAD
C7sus4b9
BASS CONT. SIM.
1.
2.
Gb7
G7#9
C-7
Gb7
G7#9
Ab7
G7#9
C7sus4b9
W/INTRO RIFF

IN WALKED BUD

-THELONIOUS MONK

(MED.-UP SWING)

INDIANA
(BACK HOME AGAIN IN INDIANA)

(UP SWING)

—JAMES F. HANLEY / BALLARD MACDONA

F Eb7 D7 G7

G–7 C7 F6 F7

Bb B°7 F D7

G7 G–7 C7

F Eb7 D7 G7

A7 D– Bb–7

F A7 D– D–/C B°7

A–7 D–7 G–7 C7 F6 (G–7 C7)

INFANT EYES

—WAYNE SHORTER

G-7 F-7 E♭maj7 A7♭9

G♭maj7 C-7/F E♭-7 F-7/B♭ B♭7♯5(♯9)

E♭maj7 Emaj7/E♭ E♭maj7♯11 Emaj7/E♭

Bmaj7 F-7/B♭ A♭-7 B♭-7/E♭ D7♭9

G-7 F-7 E♭maj7 A7♭9

G♭maj7 C-7/F E♭-7 F-7/B♭

ISLAND BIRDIE
(CALYPSO)
-McCoy Tyner
Eb F-7 Bb7 G-7 C7 F-7 Bb7
D-7b5 G7 C-7 F7 F-7 Bb7 Eb
Ab7 Gb-7 Cb7 Gb-7 Cb7
Ab7 F-7 Bb7 Gb-7 Cb7
Ab7 Bb7 N.C.

(MED.)

IT ALL DEPENDS ON YOU

-B.G. DESYLVA/LEW BROWN/RAY HENDERSON

(MED.)

IT COULD HAPPEN TO YOU

– JAMES VAN HEUSEN / JOHNNY BURKE

(BALLAD)

IT MIGHT AS WELL BE SPRING

– RICHARD RODGERS / OSCAR HAMMERSTEIN II

194
(BALLAD)
IT NEVER ENTERED MY MIND
-RICHARD RODGERS/LORENZ HART
Fmaj7 Fmaj7#5 F6 Fmaj7#5 F A-7 Ab7 G-7 C7
Fmaj7 Bbmaj7 F/A D7 1. G7sus4 G7 G-7 C7
2. G7sus4 G7 G-7 C7 Fmaj7 D-7 G-7 C7
Fmaj7 D-7 G-7 C7 Fmaj7 G-7 A-7 Abo7
G-7 C7 Fmaj7 Fmaj7#5 F6 Fmaj7#5
F A-7 Ab7 G-7 C7 Fmaj7 Bbmaj7 A-7b5 D7b9
G-7 C7 A-7 D7 G-7 C7sus4 F6 (C7)

(FAST)

IT'S A MOST UNUSUAL DAY

-JIMMY McHUGH/HAROLD ADAMSON

F#/G G E-7 A-7 D7 F#/G G

E-7 A-7 D7 G/B Cmaj7 C#o7 G/D

1. B-7 E-7 A7 D7 2. A-7 D7 G6

E-7 Eb-7 D-7 G7 Cmaj7 C6 E-7 Eb-7 D-7 G7

Cmaj7 C6 F#-7 F-7 E-7 A7 Dmaj7 D6 A-7

D7 A-7 D7 F#/G G E-7 A-7 D7

F#/G G E-7 A-7 D7 G/B Cmaj7 C#o7

G/D B-7 E-7 A7 D7 B-7 Cmaj7

B-7 Cmaj7 B-7 A-7 D7b9 G6 (A-7 D7)

(UP)

IT'S A GOOD DAY

—PEGGY LEE/
DAVE BARBOUR

F-7 B♭7 E♭6
E♭7 A♭
F7 B♭7 B♭7♯5
E♭6 E°7 B♭7/F E°7
B♭7 E°7 B♭7 B♭7♯5
E♭6 F-7 G-7 C-7
F-7 B♭7 E♭6 B♭7♯5
E♭6 F-7 G-7 C-7
F-7 B♭7 E♭6 (F-7 B♭7)

IT'S IMPOSSIBLE (SOMOS NOVIOS)

(MED. BALLAD)

-ARMANDO MANZANERO/ SID WAYNE

(MED.) # IT'S ONLY A PAPER MOON

—HAROLD ARLEN/
BILLY ROSE/
E. Y. HARBURG

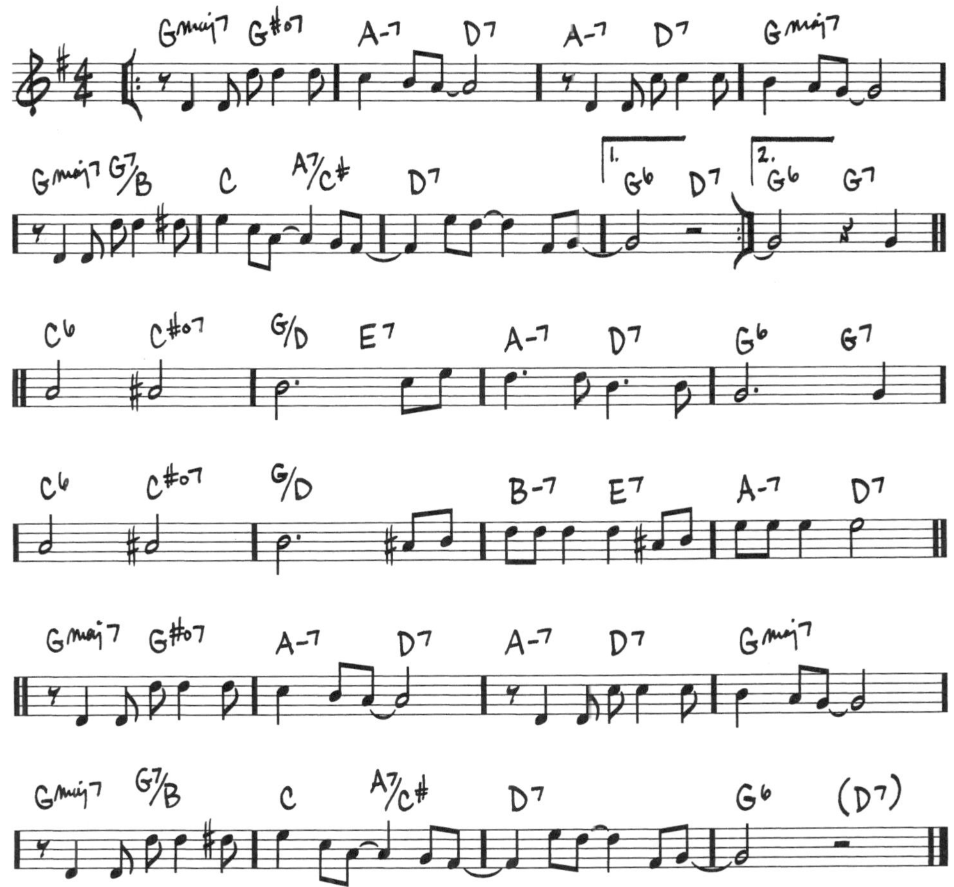

(SLOW SWING)

IT'S SO PEACEFUL IN THE COUNTRY

- ALEC WILDER

JACKIE

(BRIGHT BLUES)

—HAMPTON HAWES

JAMBA

- JACK WILKINS

(SAMBA ♩=134)

(𝅗𝅥 = 152 EVEN 8ths)

JAMES

– PAT METHENY / LYLE MAYS

JINGLES

(UP)

—JOHN L. (WES) MONTGOMER

A

E-7 A7 E-7 A7

E-7 A7 G7 Cmaj7

F♯-7 G♯-7 G7 Cmaj7

F♯-7♭5 B7♭9 E-7 A7 1. 2.

B

A-7 D7 Gmaj7 A♭-7 D♭7 G-7 C7 Fmaj7 B7 N.C.

D.S. AL 2nd ENDING

FORM A A B A

SOLOS

E-7 8 A-7 4 F♯-7♭5 B7♭9 E-7

A-7 D7 Gmaj7 A♭-7 D♭7 G-7 C7 Fmaj7 F♯-7♭5 B7♭9

E-7 8 A-7 4 F♯-7♭5 B7♭9 E-7

(MED.)

JITTERBUG WALTZ

—THOMAS "FATS" WALLER

(FUNKY BLUES)

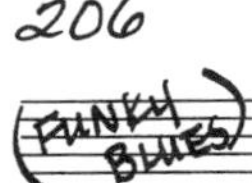

THE JODY GRIND

— HORACE SILVER

Bb-7
Eb7
Bb-7
3
A13
B13
Bb-7
1.
3
2.
3

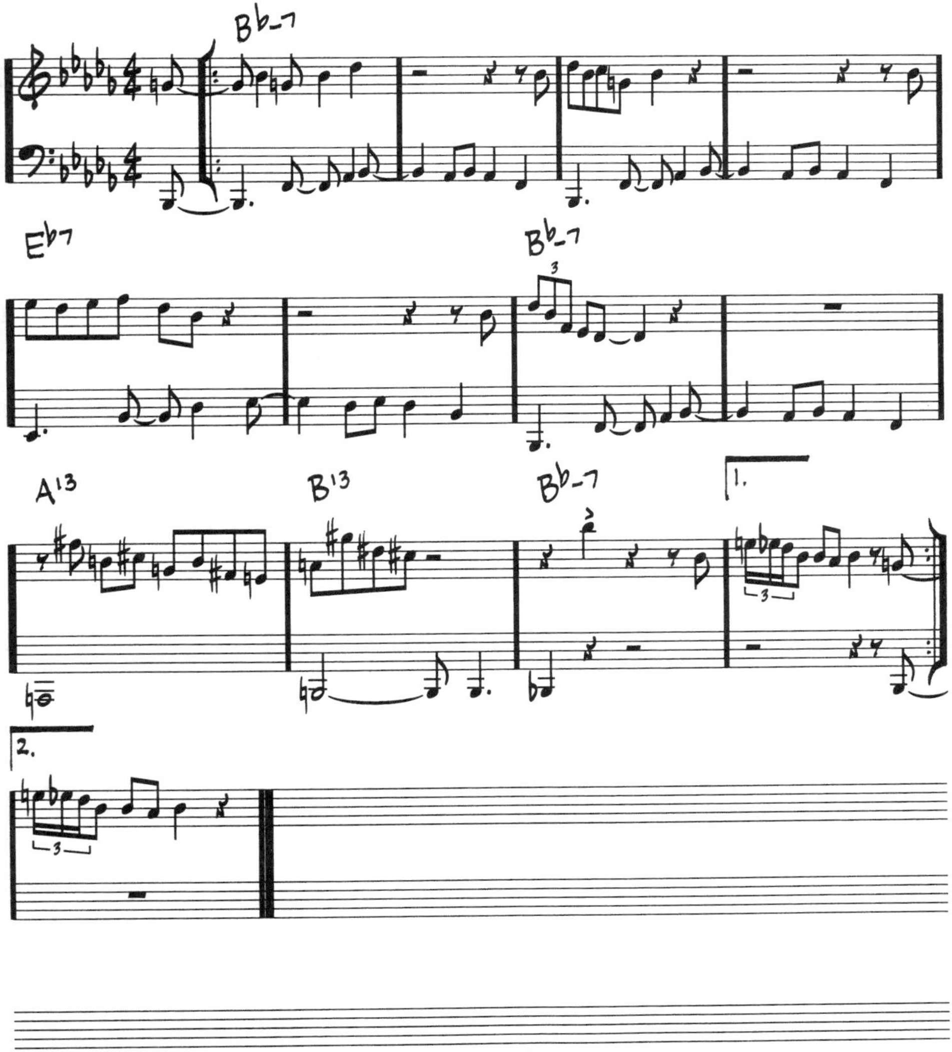

(MED. UP) **JUMPIN' WITH SYMPHONY SID**

— LESTER YOUNG / BUDDY FEYNE

(MED. FAST)

JUNE IS BUSTIN' OUT ALL OVER

—RICHARD RODGERS/OSCAR HAMMERSTEIN II

(UP)

JUST A FEW

– SHORTY ROGERS

JUST THE TWO OF US
- RALPH MACDONALD / WILLIAM SALTER / BILL WITHERS
(MED. ROCK/LATIN)
♩=96
INTRO
Dbmaj7 C7 F-7 Eb-7 Ab7
Dbmaj7 C7 F-7 Dbmaj7 C7#5
F-7 Eb-7 Ab7 Dbmaj7 C7#5 F-7
A
Dbmaj7 C7 F-7 Eb-7 Ab7 Dbmaj7 C7 F-7
Dbmaj7 C7 F-7 Eb-7 Ab7 Dbmaj7 C7 F-7
B
Dbmaj7 C7 F-7 E-7 Eb-7 Ab7 Dbmaj7 C7 F-7
Dbmaj7 C7 F-7 E-7 Eb-7 Ab7 Dbmaj7 C7 F-7

C
Dbmaj7
C7sus4
C7
Cbmaj7
Bb7sus4
Bb7
Amaj7
Ab7sus4
Ab7
1.
Dbmaj7
Gb13
2.
Dbmaj7
Gb13
Dbmaj7
C7
F-7
Eb-7
Ab7
Dbmaj7
C7
F-7
D.S. AL
F-7
D
Dbmaj7
C7
F-7
E-7
Eb-7
Ab7
Dbmaj7
C7
F-7
Dbmaj7
C7
F-7
E-7
Eb-7
Ab7
Dbmaj7
C7
F-7
REPEAT AND FADE

KARY'S TRANCE

(MED. UP)

-LEE KONITZ

(JAZZ WALTZ)

KATRINA BALLERINA

-WOODY SHAW

(MED. SWING)

KICKIN' THE GONG AROUND

—TED KOEHLER/HAROLD ARLEN

A

F- C7 F- C7 F- C7 F- C7

F- C7 F- C7 F- C7 F- D7

G- D7 G- D7 G- D7 G- C7

F- C7 F- C7 F- C7 F- C7

B

F6 Bb-7 F6 Bb-7 F6

Db9 C9 Db9 C9 F6 C7

F6 Bb-7 F6 Bb-7 F7

Db9 C9 Db9 C9 F6
(SOLOS C7 F6) E7
C
A6 E7
C6 G7 C7
D
F6 Bb-7 F6 Bb-7 F6
Db9 C9 Db9 C9 F6
FINE
SOLOS ON B
AFTER SOLOS, D.S. AL FINE

KIDS ARE PRETTY PEOPLE

(MED. SLOW)

– THAD JONES

AFTER SOLOS, LAST HEAD, VAMP INTRO TILL FADE

LADY DAY

-WAYNE SHORTER

(UP)

THE LADY IS A TRAMP

- RICHARD RODGERS/ LORENZ HART

LAKES
-PAT METHENY
(♩=180 EVEN 8ths)
INTRO
HEAD
SOLOS
(last x)
FINE
AFTER SOLOS, D.S. AL FINE

(BALLAD)

LAST NIGHT WHEN WE WERE YOUNG

-HAROLD ARLEN/E.Y. HARBURG

(MED.)

THE LAST TIME I SAW PARIS

—JEROME KERN/OSCAR HAMMERSTEIN

(MED. SWING)

LEARNIN' THE BLUES

–DOLORES "VICKI" SILVERS

LEILA

(SLOW SWING)

JOHN L. (WES) MONTGOMERY

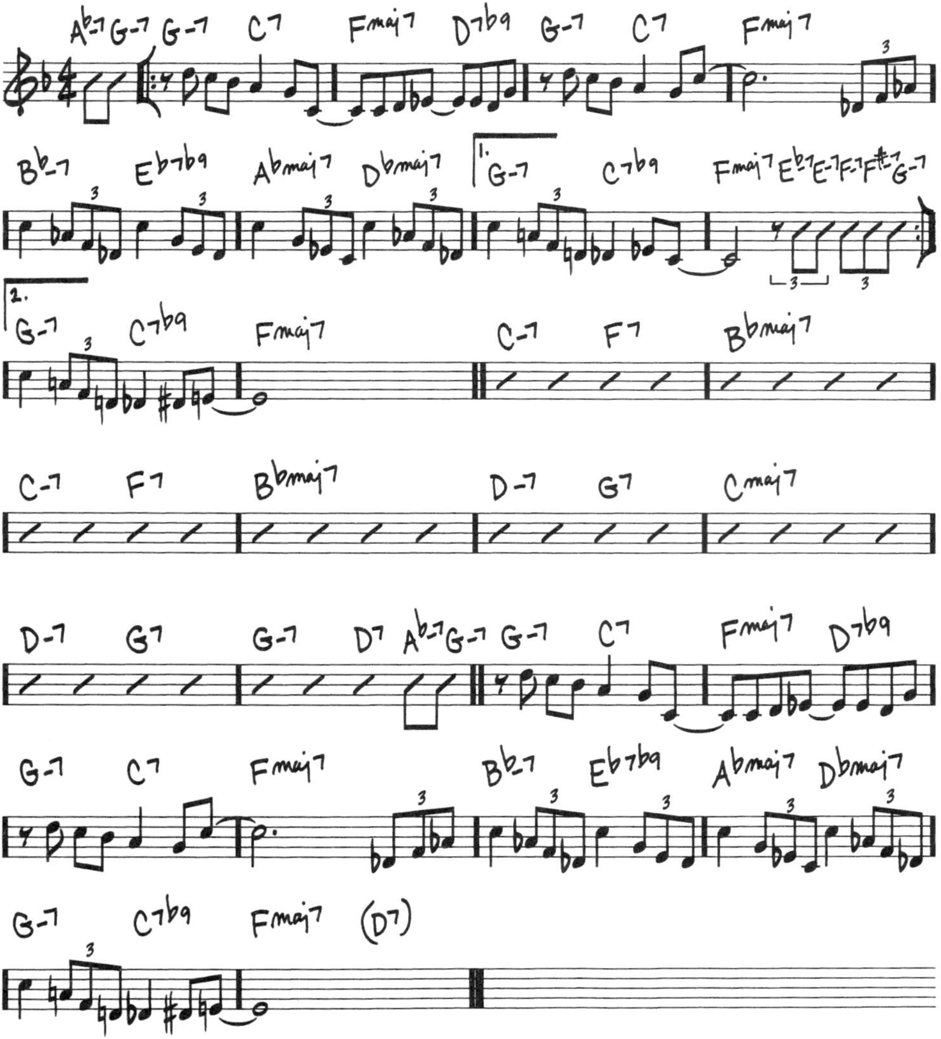
A♭-7 G-7 G-7 C7 Fmaj7 D7♭9 G-7 C7 Fmaj7
B♭-7 E♭7♭9 A♭maj7 D♭maj7 1. G-7 C7♭9 Fmaj7 E♭-7 E-7 F-7 F♯-7 G-7
2. G-7 C7♭9 Fmaj7 C-7 F7 B♭maj7
C-7 F7 B♭maj7 D-7 G7 Cmaj7
D-7 G7 G-7 D7 A♭-7 G-7 G-7 C7 Fmaj7 D7♭9
G-7 C7 Fmaj7 B♭-7 E♭7♭9 A♭maj7 D♭maj7
G-7 C7♭9 Fmaj7 (D7)

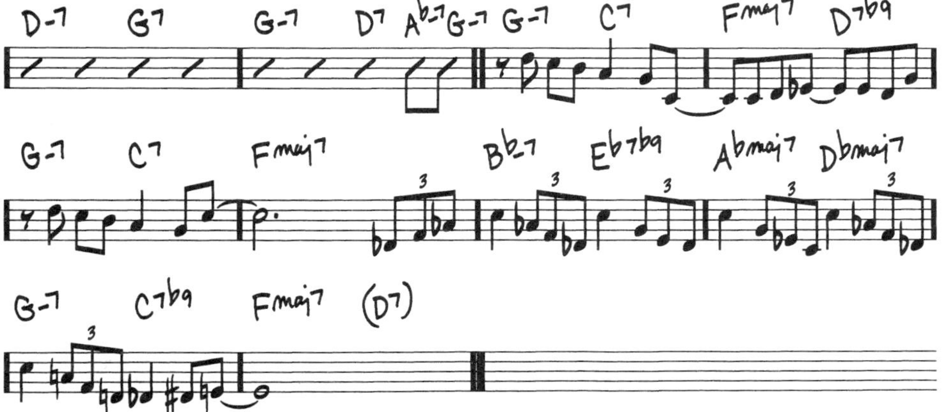

(FAST SWING)

LENNIE'S PENNIES

- LENNIE TRISTANO

(MED.)

LET THERE BE LOVE

-LIONEL RAND/
IAN GRANT

(MED. SWING)
LET'S COOL ONE
—THELONIOUS MONK
Ebmaj7 F-7 Bb7 Ebmaj7 D7b5 Db7 G7 C7b5(b9)
F7 1. Bb7 Eb6 (DRUM FILL) (F-7 Bb7)
2. Bb7 Eb6 (DRUM FILL)
Bb-7 Eb7 Abmaj7
3
F7(11) Bb7 sus 4
Ebmaj7 F-7 Bb7 Ebmaj7 D7b5 Db7 G7 C7b5(b9)
F7 Bb7 Eb6 (DRUM FILL)
AFTER SOLOS, D.C. AL
(TAKE REPEAT)
Bb7 Eb6 (DRUM FILL)

LET'S GET LOST

—JIMMY MCHUGH/
FRANK LOESSER

(MED.)

LIKE SONNY
(SIMPLE LIKE)

-JOHN COLTRANE

(LATIN)

D-7 F-7

Ab-7 Bb7b9

Ebmaj7 A-7

F-7

C#-7 F#7 Bmaj7

Eb-7 Ab7 D-7

F-7 Ab-7

Bb7b9 Ebmaj7

(LAST X)

LIKE YOUNG

-PAUL WEBSTER/ ANDRE PREVIN

(MED. BLUES)

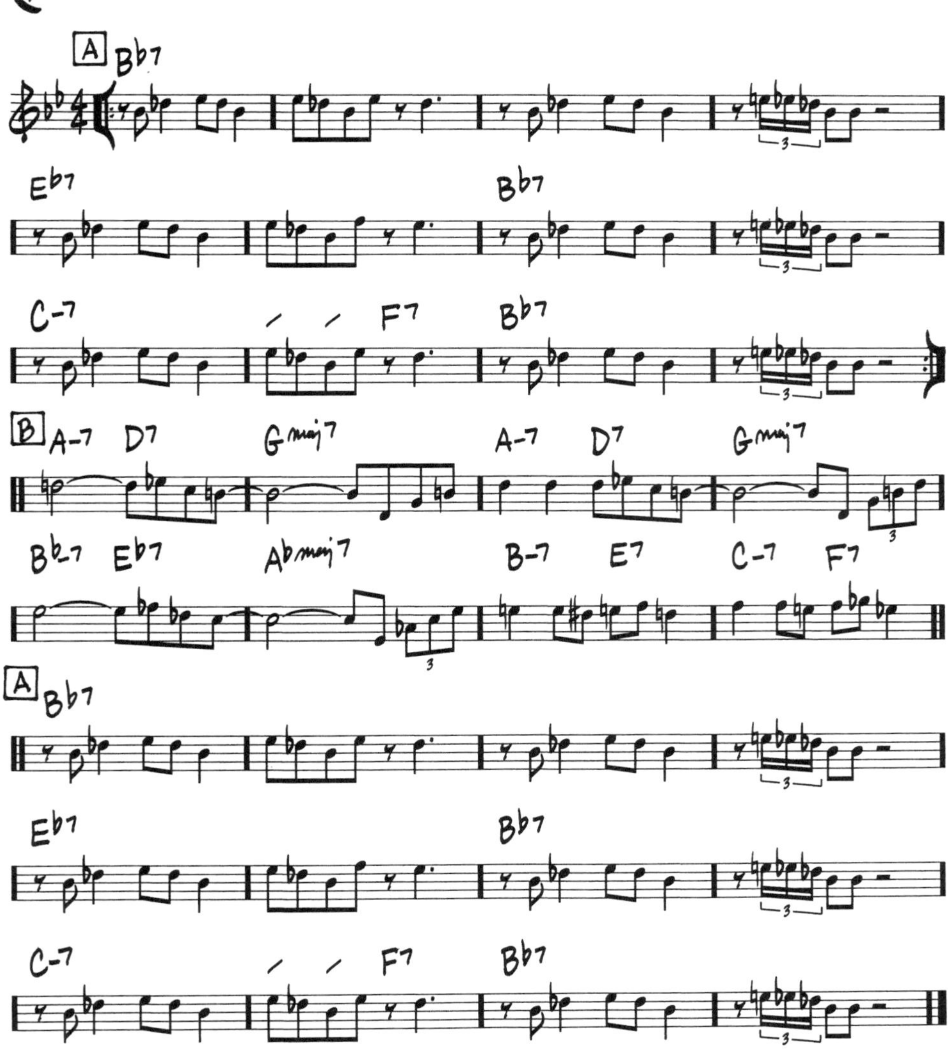

LIMBO

(UP (EVEN 8THS))

— WAYNE SHORTER

Eb-7 | Gb7sus4 | Cmaj7 | F7sus4

Bb7sus4 | Dmaj7 | G/Ab |

Abmaj7 | Gbmaj7 | Gb7sus4 | Gmaj7#11 Gbmaj7#11

Fmaj7#11 Emaj7#11 | C#-7 | A7 | Eb-7

D7#11

232
FAST
LINE GAMES
- PAT MARTINO
(DRUM FILLS)
A
N.C.
(UNISON)
A sus4
/B
B
D/E
C/D
C maj9
B♭6
A-11
A/G
SOLOS ON B
AFTER SOLOS, D.C. (INTRO) AL

(MED.)

LINGER AWHILE

- VINCENT ROSE / HARRY OWENS

F6 C7 F6 D♭7

C7 C°7 C7

G-7 C7 C7#5(#9)

Fmaj7 F°7 Fmaj7 C7

D-7 A7

D7 G7 G-7 C7

F6 C7 F6 D♭7

C7 F6 (G-7 C7)

(♩=216 FAST)

LITTLE CHICAGO FIRE

-FRANK FOSTER

LITTLE ROOTIE TOOTIE

(MED. SWING)

—THELONIOUS MONK

236
♩=88 (EVEN 8ths)
LITTLE SHOES
-MIKE STERN
*PLAY ON D.C. ONLY
SIM.
1ST X - TO SOLOS
AFTER D.S. - D.C. AL ⊕
(NO REPEAT ON B)
Copyright © 1986 Little Shoes Music (ASCAP)

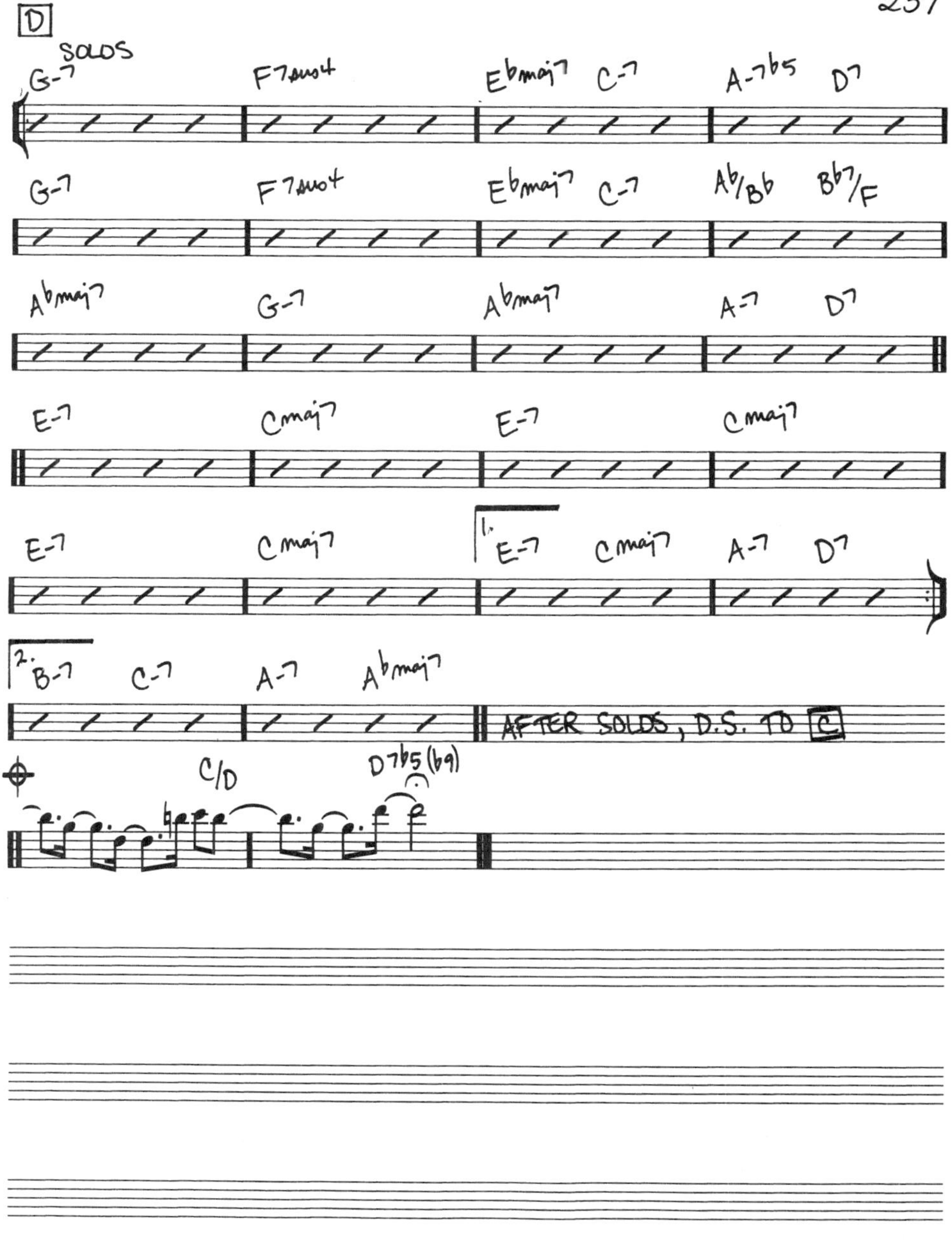

D

SOLOS

G-7 | F7sus4 | E♭maj7 C-7 | A-7♭5 D7

G-7 | F7sus4 | E♭maj7 C-7 | A♭/B♭ B♭7/F

A♭maj7 | G-7 | A♭maj7 | A-7 D7

E-7 | Cmaj7 | E-7 | Cmaj7

E-7 | Cmaj7 | 1. E-7 Cmaj7 | A-7 D7

2. B-7 C-7 | A-7 A♭maj7

AFTER SOLOS, D.S. TO C

C/D D7♭5(♭9)

(MED. LATIN)
LITTLE SUNFLOWER
-FREDDIE HUBBARD
INTRO
(BASS) D-
HEAD
D-7
BASS CONTINUE SIMILE
1.
2.
E♭maj7
Dmaj7
1.
2.
D-7
TAKE REPEATS ON SOLOS
AFTER SOLOS, LAST HEAD, VAMP INTRO TO FADE

LONELY DREAMS

(BALLAD)

—TERRY GIBBS

240
LONE JACK
-PAT METHENY/
LYLE MAYS
(SAMBA ♩=176)
A
Bb-7
Gbmaj7
Bb-7
Gbmaj7
Bb-7
Gbmaj7
F7#9
Ab
Bb-
1.
2.
B
Eb-7
Dbmaj7
Cbmaj7
Bb-7
Dbmaj7/Ab
Gbmaj7
F7#9
Ab
Bb-
D.S. AL
C
Db/Eb
Eb/F
Gb/Ab
F/G
Db/Eb
Eb/F
Bb/C
Ab/Bb

D/E E/F# G/A A/B C/D D/E F/G G/A Ab/Bb
SOLOS
Gbmaj7 Bb-7 Gbmaj7
Bb-7 Gbmaj7 F7#9 Ab Bb-
Bb-7 Gbmaj7 Bb-7 Gbmaj7
Bb-7 Gbmaj7 F7#9 Ab Bb-
Eb-7 F7b9 Gbmaj7 G-7b5
G-7/C C7 Ab-7/Db Db7 Bb-7/Eb Eb7 C-7/F F7
Bb-7 Gbmaj7 Bb-7 Gbmaj7
Bb-7 Gbmaj7 F7#9 Ab Bb-
AFTER SOLOS, D.S. AL ⊕ 2
(TAKE REPEAT AND 1ST D.S)
⊕ 2
(ENDING)
Db/Eb Eb/F Gb/Ab F/G
Db/Eb Eb/F Bb/C Ab/Bb D/E E/F# G/A A/B
C/D D/E F/G
(FILL)

(MED.)

LOOK FOR THE SILVER LINING

–JEROME KERN / BUDDY DESYLVA

Ebmaj7 | F-7 Bb7 | Ebmaj7 | F-7 Bb7 |

Ebmaj7 | Ab7 | G-7 | C-7 |

F-7 | Bb7 | Ebmaj7 | D-7b5 G7#9 |

C-7 | F7 F#o7 | G-7 C7 | F-7 Bb7 ||

Ebmaj7 | F-7 Bb7 | Ebmaj7 | F-7 Bb7 |

Bb-7 | Eb7 | Abmaj7 | Ab6 |

F7 | F#o7 | G-7 | C7 |

F-7 | Bb7 | Ebmaj7 | (F-7 Bb7) ||

(BALLAD)

LOOK TO THE RAINBOW

– BURTON LANE / E. Y. HARBURG

(BALLAD)

LOST IN THE STARS

- KURT WEILL/MAXWELL ANDERSON

C-7 F7
Bbmaj7 G-7
C-7b5 F7
E7 Eb7 D7
Gmaj7 Bbo7
A-7 D7
Gmaj7 E7#5
A-7 D7
Gmaj7 G7sus4
C6 F7
Gmaj7 G7sus4
C6 F7
D7
Gmaj7
E-7 Eb7
Gmaj7 Bbo7
D7
Gmaj7
E-7 Eb7
Gmaj7 Bbo7
D7
Gmaj7 (A-7 D7)

(MED.)

LOVE IS JUST AROUND THE CORNER

—LEO ROBIN/LEWIS E. GENSLER

(MED. BALLAD)

LOVE, LOOK AWAY

—RICHARD RODGERS/OSCAR HAMMERSTEIN II

LOVE VIBRATIONS

–HORACE SILVER

(BOSSA)

(BALLAD) A LOVELY WAY TO SPEND AN EVENING

-JIMMY McHUGH/HAROLD ADAMSON

LOVER

– RICHARD RODGERS / LORENZ HART

(MED. UP)

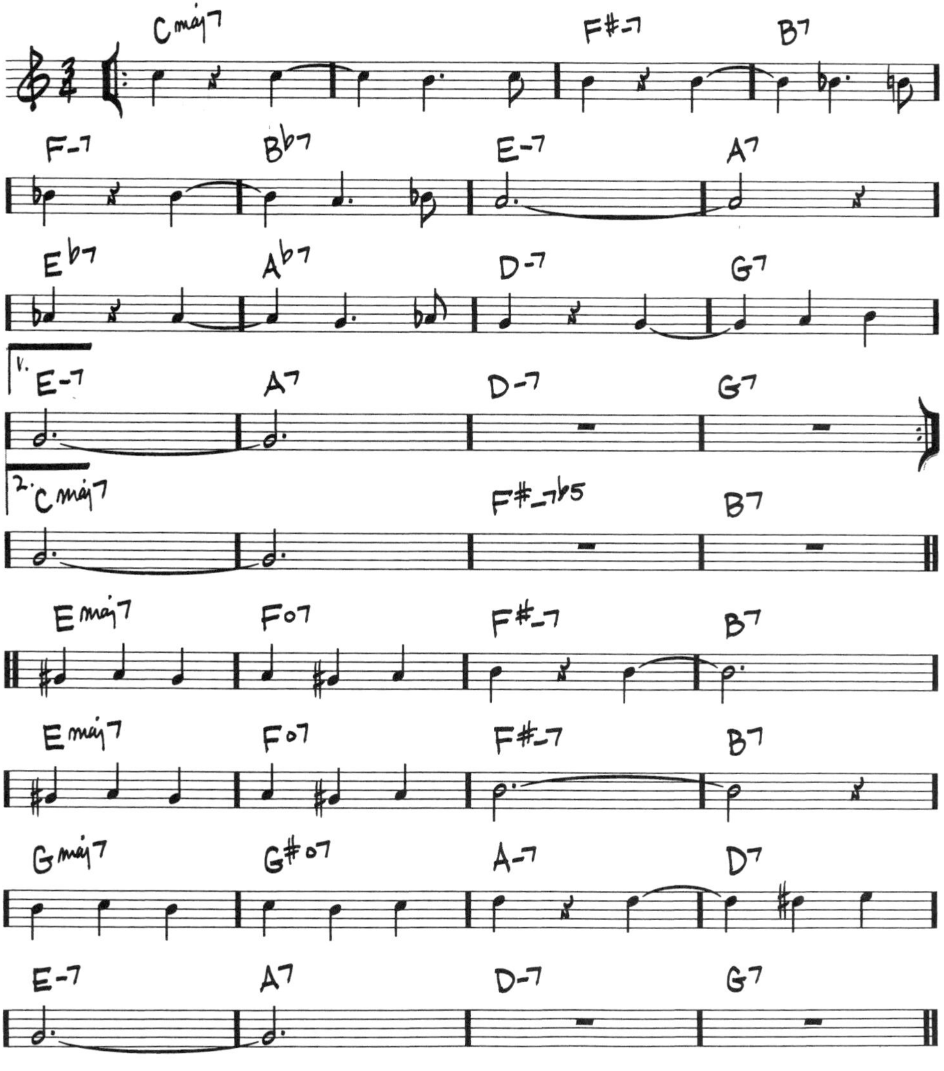

Cmaj7 | | F#–7 | B7 |

F–7 | B♭7 | E–7 | A7 |

E♭7 | A♭7 | D–7 | G7 |

1. E–7 | A7 | D–7 | G7 :‖

2. Cmaj7 | | F#–7♭5 | B7 ‖

Emaj7 | F°7 | F#–7 | B7 |

Emaj7 | F°7 | F#–7 | B7 |

Gmaj7 | G#°7 | A–7 | D7 |

E–7 | A7 | D–7 | G7 ‖

Cmaj7
F#-7
B7
F-7
Bb7
E-7
A7
Eb-7
Ab7
D-7
G7
C6
(A-7
D-7
G7)

(UP)

LOVER, COME BACK TO ME

- SIGMUND ROMBERG / OSCAR HAMMERSTEIN II

G-7 C7 F#-7 B7 E- E-(maj7) E-7 E-6
F#-7b5 B7b9 E-7 A7
A-7 D7 G6
F#-7b5 B7b9 E-7
B-7b5 E7b9 A-7 A-7/G
F9#11 E-7 Eb9#11 D7 G6 G6/B C6 C#o7
G6 (E-7 A-7 D7b9)

LOVER MAN (OH, WHERE CAN YOU BE?)

(BALLAD)

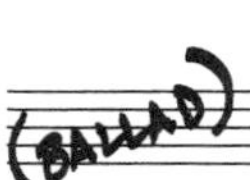

–JIMMY DAVIS/ ROGER RAMIREZ/ JIMMY SHERMAN

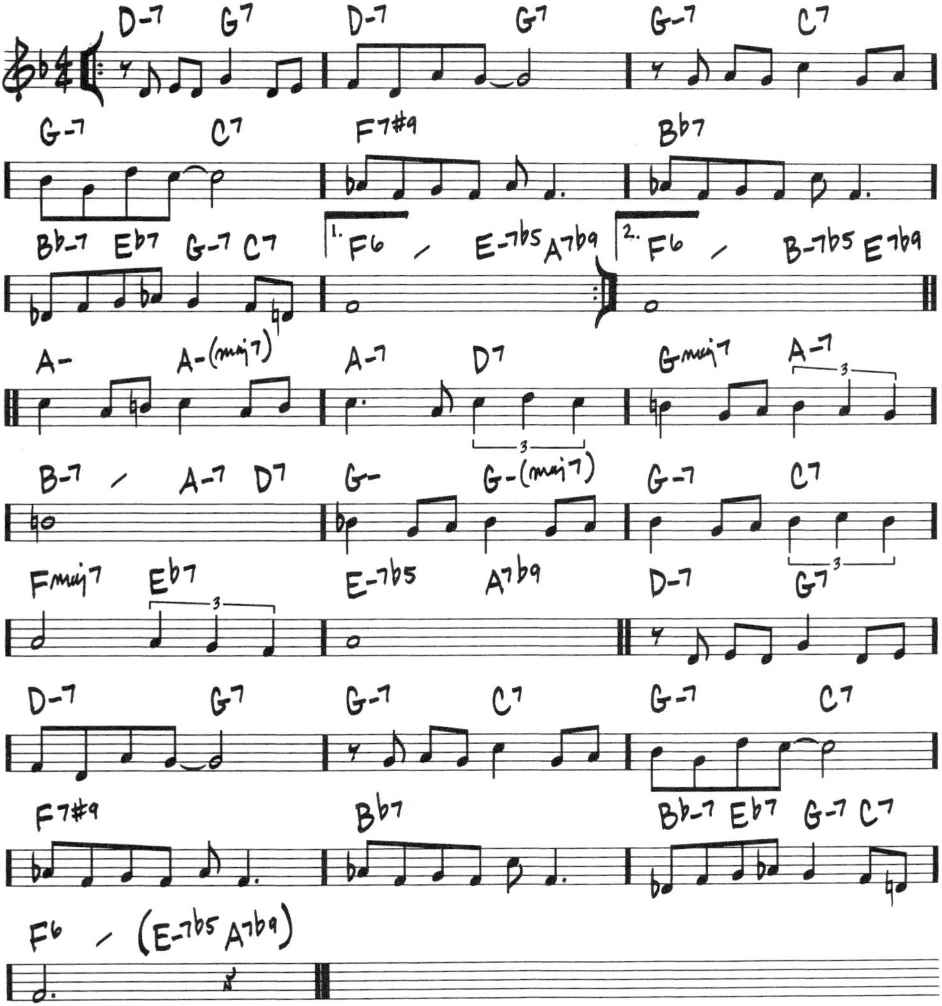

MANHATTAN

- RICHARD RODGERS/ LORENZ HART

(MED.)

MANTECA

–DIZZY GILLESPIE/
WALTER GIL FULLER/
LUCIANO POZO GONZALES

(MED. LATIN)

MASQUERADE

– JOHN JACOB LOEB/
PAUL FRANCIS WEBSTER

(MED.)

Gmaj7 Bbo7 D7

Gmaj7 Bbo7 D7

Gmaj7 A- E7 A- D7b9

G6 A-7/D G6 1. A-7/D 2. (G6) F#7

B-

Go7

D

E9 A7 D7 Ab9#11

D.C. AL CODA

G6 A-7/D G6 (A-7 D7)

SOLO ON ENTIRE FORM

(I'M AFRAID) THE MASQUERADE IS OVER

-ALLIE WRUBEL/
HERB MAGIDSON

(MED.)

Ebmaj7 D-7b5 G7#9 C-7 F7 Bb-7 Eb7

Abmaj7 G-7 C7 F7 F-7 Bb7 Ebmaj7 Bb-7 Eb7

Abmaj7 Db9 1. G-7 C7 F-7 Bb7

2. G-7 C7 F-7 Bb7 Eb6 Db9 Eb9 F-7 Bb7 Ebmaj7 C-7

F-7 Bb7 Ebmaj7 A-7b5 D7 G-7 C7 C-7 F7 F-7 Bb7

Ebmaj7 D-7b5 G7#9 C-7 F7 Bb-7 Eb7

Abmaj7 G-7 C7 F7 F-7 Bb7

Ebmaj7 Bb-7 Eb7 Abmaj7 Db9

G-7 C7 F-7 Bb7sus4 Eb6 (F-7 Bb7)

(MED.)

MEAN TO ME

–FRED E. AHLERT/
ROY TURK

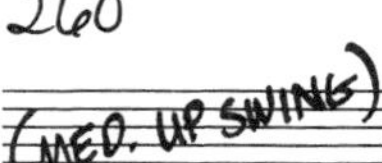

MAYREH

(MED. UP SWING)

—HORACE SILVER

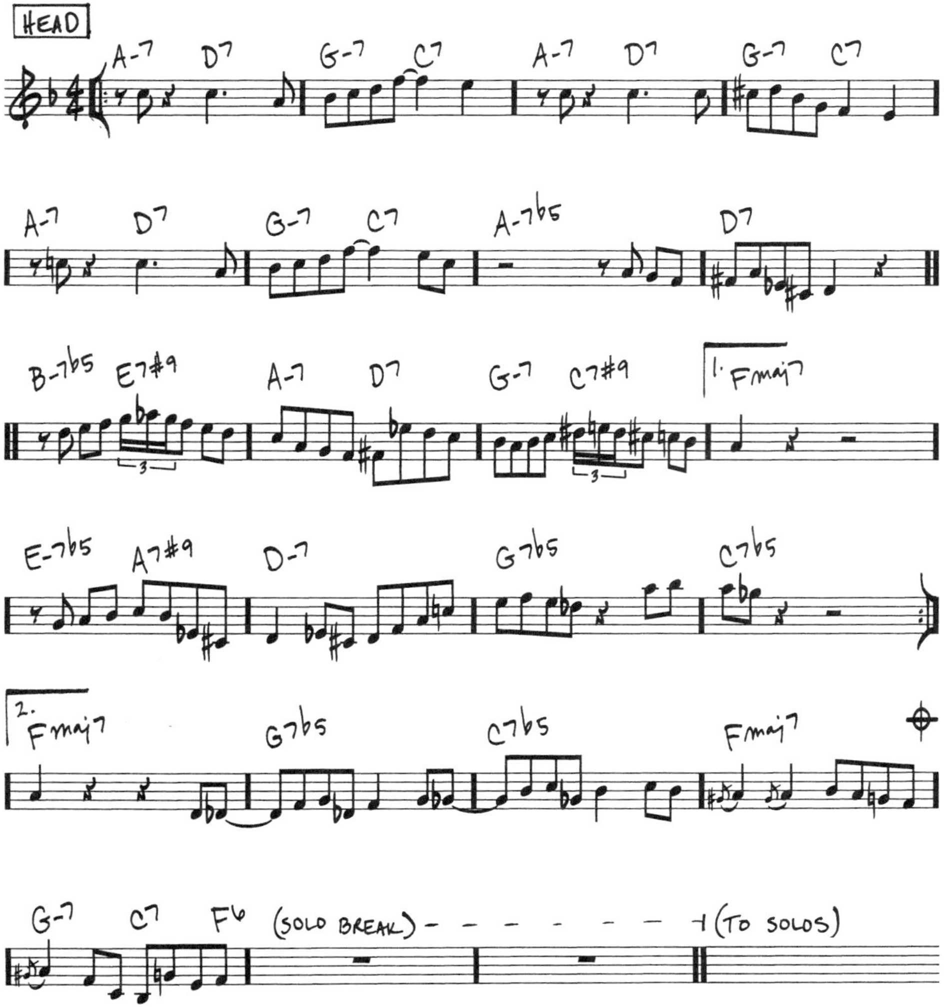
HEAD
A-7 D7 G-7 C7 A-7 D7 G-7 C7
A-7 D7 G-7 C7 A-7♭5 D7
B-7♭5 E7#9 A-7 D7 G-7 C7#9
1. Fmaj7
E-7♭5 A7#9 D-7 G7♭5 C7♭5
2. Fmaj7 G7♭5 C7♭5 Fmaj7
G-7 C7 F6 (SOLO BREAK)
(TO SOLOS)
3
3

SOLOS
Fmaj7 D7b9 G-7 C7 Fmaj7 D7b9 G-7 C7
Fmaj7 D7b9 G-7 C7 A-7b5 D7b9
B-7b5 E7b9 A-7 D7 G-7 C7 Fmaj7
1. E-7b5 A7b9 D-7 G7 C7
2. G7 C7 Fmaj7 G-7 C7
AFTER SOLOS, D.C. AL ⊕
G-7 C7 Bbmaj7 A7#5 F-/Ab G7 Gbmaj7 N.C.
Fmaj7

(Bossa)

MENINA FLOR

-Luiz Bonfa/
Maria Toledo

(BALLAD OR MED. SWING)

MIDNIGHT SUN

– LIONEL HAMPTON/ SONNY BURKE/ JOHNNY MERCER

(MED. SWING)

MILES AHEAD

– MILES DAVIS

Cmaj7
D-7
G-7
C7
Fmaj7
B-7b5
E7
E-7b5
A7
D-7
G7
D7
G7
D.S. FOR SOLOS
AFTER SOLOS, D.S. AL
A7
D-7
G7sus4
Bbmaj7
Db7
Cmaj7

MINOR MISHAP

(MED. UP SWING)

-TOMMY FLANAGAN

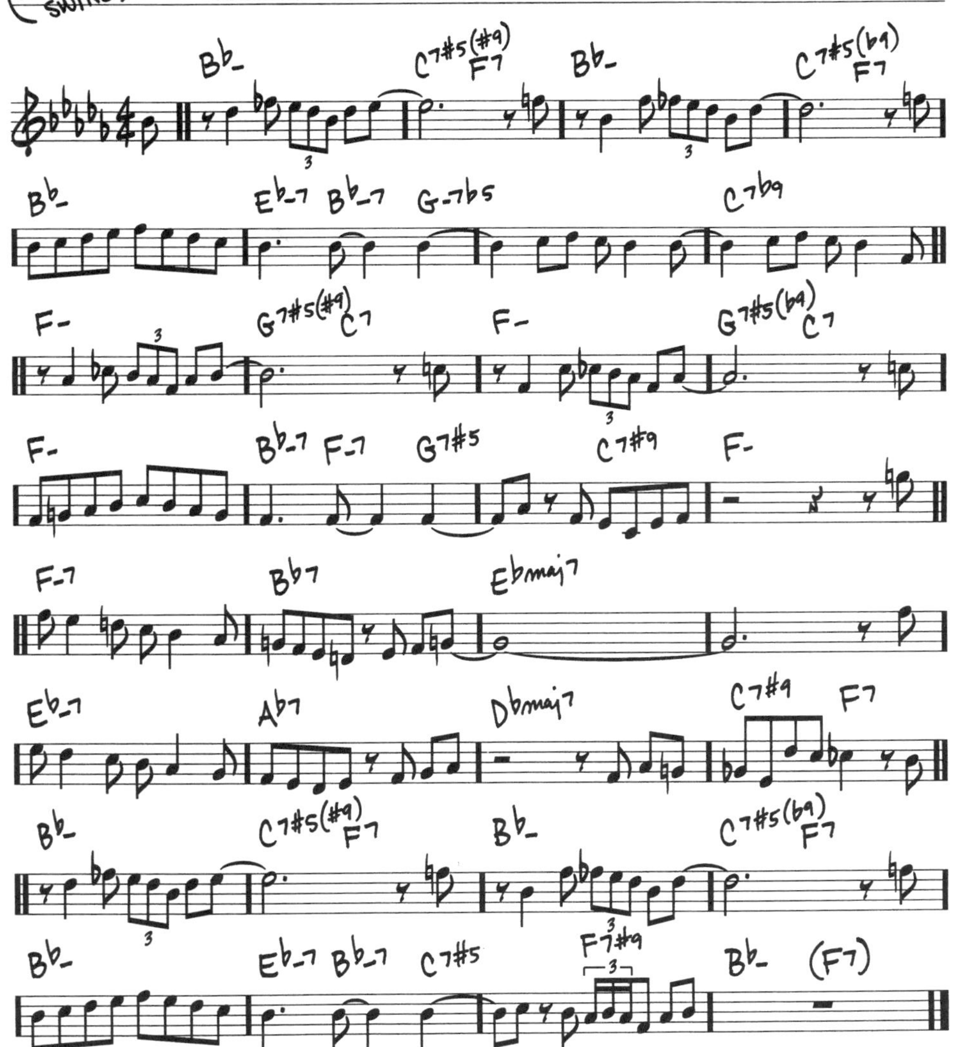

(MED.)
MINOR MOOD
– CLIFFORD BROWN
F- Bb-6 C7 F-
(Bb7) Bb-7 Eb7 G-7b5 C7#5
F- Db7 C7 F-(maj7) C7b5(#9)
F- Bb-6 C7 F-
(Bb7) Bb-7 Eb7 G-7b5 C7#5
F- Db7 C7 F-(maj7)
N.C.
(SOLO BREAK)
(SOLOS – F MINOR BLUES)
(AFTER SOLOS)
F- G-7b5 C7 F- C-7b5 F7b9 Bb-7
C7#5 G-7b5 Abmaj7 G-7b5 C7
1. F-(maj7)
2. F-(maj7)

(UP)

THEME FROM MR. BROADWAY

-DAVE BRUBECK

MR. MAGIC

—RALPH MACDONALD/
WILLIAM SALTER

(MED. SLOW)
FUNK

MOANIN'

(MED. SWING)
— BOBBY TIMMONS
A
Bb/F
F
N.C.
Bb/F
F
Bb/F
F
CONT. RHYTHM SIM.
Bb/F
F
1.
2.
B
Bb-7
Ab7
G7b9
C7#5(#9)
Bb/F
F-
B9b5
Bb-7
Ab7
G7b9
C7#5(#9)
N.C.
C
(N.C.)
Bb/F
F
Bb/F
F
(RHYTHM AS BEFORE)
Bb/F
F

Bb/F F
D SOLOS
F-6 Ab7 G7#5(b9) C7#5(#9)
2
2
2
Bb-7 Ab7 G7b9 C7#5(#9) F-6 F7 F7#5(b9)
Bb-7 Ab7 G7b9 G-7b5 C7#5
F-6 Ab7 G7#5(b9) C7#5(#9)
2
2
F-6
AFTER SOLOS, D.S. AL ⊕
TAKE REPEAT
Bb/F F
E
Bb-7 Ab7 G7b9 C7#5(#9)
Bb/F F- B9(#11) Bb-7 Ab7 G7b9 C7#5(#9) F- Db/E
Eb6(9) D7b5(#9) Dbmaj7 C7#5(#9) Bb/F F-

MONK'S MOOD

(BALLAD)

-THELONIOUS MONK

F-7 Bb7 Cmaj7 D-7b5 G7

Dbmaj7 /C /B Bb7 A7 E7b9 Eb7

1. D9sus4 E9sus4 D-7 Bb7b5(b9) 2. Ab7#5 G7 Dbmaj7

Bb/C A/C Bb/C F#-7 B7 E

A-7b5 Ab7 G7sus4 G#07 A-7b5 F7 F-7 Eb-7/Bb D-7 Bb7b5(b9)

F-7 Bb7 Cmaj7 D-7b5 G7 Dbmaj7 /C /B

Bb7 A7 E7b9 Eb7 Ab7#5 G7 Dbmaj7

MONK'S SHOP
-JOHN L. (WES) MONTGOMERY
(UP)
Abmaj7 Bb-7 C-7 Db-7
C-7 F7 Bb-7 Eb7 Abmaj7 1. Abmaj7
2. F-7 Bb7 Eb-7 Ab7 Dbmaj7 Db6 C-7 F7#9
Bb-7 F7 Bb7 Eb7 Abmaj7
Bb-7 C-7 Db-7 C-7
(C-7) F7 Bb-7 Eb7 Abmaj7
SOLOS
Abmaj7 Bb-7 Eb7 Abmaj7 Db-7 Gb7 C-7 F7 Bb-7 Eb7 Abmaj7 1. Bb-7 Eb7 2. Eb-7 Ab7
Dbmaj7 Eb-7 Ab7 Dbmaj7 C-7b5 F7 Bb-7 F7 Bb7 Eb7
Abmaj7 Bb-7 Eb7 Abmaj7 Db-7 Gb7 C-7 F7 Bb-7 Eb7 Abmaj7 Bb-7 Eb7

MOON RAYS
— HORACE SILVER
(MED. LATIN)
A
F-7 Bb7 Ebmaj7 F#-7
Bb PEDAL
*(B7) F-7 *(Bb7) F-7 A-7b5 Ab-(maj7) Ab-7 G-7b5
*ON SOLOS
C7b9 F-7 Bb7 Ebmaj7 Ebmaj7/Ab
1. Ebmaj7 Ebmaj7/Ab
2. Ebmaj7 Ebmaj7/Ab
B
A-7 D7 Gmaj7
D PEDAL
Bb-7 Eb7 A-7 D7
A-7 C#-7b5 C-(maj7) C-7 B-7b5 E7b9
A-7 D7b9 G-7 C7 F-7 Bb7
D.S. AL
Ebmaj7 Ebmaj7/Ab
FINE
SOLO ON ENTIRE FORM A A B A
SOLOS SWING - NO PEDALS

MOON RIVER

(BALLAD)

— HENRY MANCINI / JOHNNY MERCER

MOONGLOW

(MED. BALLAD)

-WILL HUDSON/
EDDIE DE LANGE/
IRVING MILLS

MOOSE THE MOOCHE

— CHARLIE PARKER

(BOP)

(BALLAD)

MORE THAN YOU KNOW

—VINCENT YOUMANS
WILLIAM ROSE/
EDWARD ELISCU

(MED. SAMBA/FUNK)
MORNING DANCE
-JAY BECKENSTEIN
A
F
F/A
Bb-7
Eb7
Bbmaj7
C9sus4
1.
D-7
G7sus4
G7
C13sus4
2.
B
Ebmaj9(#11)
G-7
E-7b5
Eb7b5
C7
AFTER SOLOS, D.C. AL
C#9sus4
F#(VAMP)
F#/A#
B-7
E7
REPEAT AND FADE

MOTEN SWING

(MED. SWING)

—BUSTER MOTEN/
BENNIE MOTEN

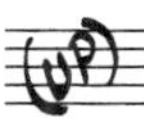

MOVE

— DENZIL DE COSTA BEST

(UP)

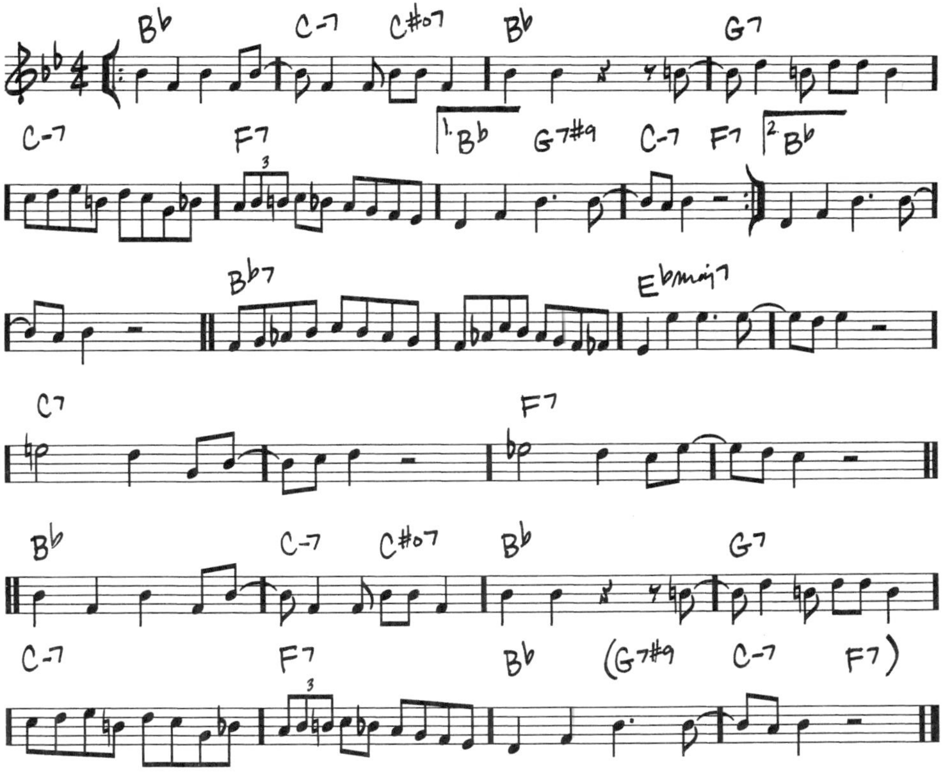
Bb C-7 C#o7 Bb G7
C-7 F7 1. Bb G7#9 C-7 F7 2. Bb
Bb7 Ebmaj7
C7 F7
Bb C-7 C#o7 Bb G7
C-7 F7 Bb (G7#9 C-7 F7)

(MED. SAMBA)
MY ATTORNEY BERNIE
-DAVE FRISHBERG
D-7b5 D-7b5/G
C#o7
N.C.
F-7
Bb7
Eb-7
Ab7
Dbmaj7
Gbmaj7
C-7
F7b9
A-7
D7
G7
Ab7(#11)
F9sus4
Bbmaj7
D9sus4
Gmaj7
D7#5
G-
F-9
Bb13
(FILL)
Eb
D7#9
Gadd9
AFTER SOLOS, D.S. AL
D7b9
G-6

(MED.)

MY BLUE HEAVEN

-WALTER DONALDSON/GEORGE WHITING

⊕ F7 B♭7 E♭6

284
(BALLAD OR MED. SWING)
MY HEART STOOD STILL
-RICHARD RODGERS/LORENZ HART
F6 D-7 G-7 C7 Fmaj7 F7 Bb6 Eb7
A-7 D7 G-7 C7 1. A-7 D7b9 G-7 C7
2. F6 F-7 Bb7
G7b9 Cmaj7 D-7b5 G7
Db7 C7 F6 D-7 G-7 C7
Fmaj7 F7 Bb6 Eb7 A-7 D-7 G-7 C7
F6 (D-7 G-7 C7)

MY LITTLE SUEDE SHOES

(MED. LATIN)

—CHARLIE PARKER

F-7 Bb7 Eb6 C-7 F-7 Bb7 Eb6 C-7

F-7 Bb7 G-7 C7 F-7 Bb7 1. Eb6

2. Eb6 Ab6 G-7 C7 F-7 Bb7 Eb6

Ab6 G-7 C7 F-7 Bb7 Eb6

F-7 Bb7 Eb6 C-7 F-7 Bb7 Eb6 C-7

F-7 Bb7 G-7 C7 F-7 Bb7 Eb6

MY OLD FLAME

(BALLAD)

- ARTHUR JOHNSTON / SAM COSLOW

(MED.)

MY SILENT LOVE

–DANA SUESSE/
EDWARD HEYMAN

(BALLAD)

THE NEARNESS OF YOU

– HOAGY CARMICHAEL/
NED WASHINGTON

(BALLAD) A NIGHTINGALE SANG IN BERKELEY SQUARE

— MANNING SHERWIN / ERIC MASCHWITZ

(MED.)
NIGHT SONG
-LEE ADAMS/
CHARLES STROUSE
(LATIN)
Fmaj7
F6
Fmaj7
F6
Fmaj7
F6
C-7
F7
(SWING)
Bbmaj7
Bb-6
A-7
D7#9
G-7
C7
F6
1.
G-7
C7
2.
F7#9
(LATIN)
Bb-7
Eb7
Ab6
3
D-7
G7
C6
(LATIN)
A7

G-7
C7
(LATIN)
Fmaj7
F6
Fmaj7
F6
Fmaj7
F6
C-7
F7
(SWING)
Bbmaj7
Bb-6
A-7
D7#9
G-7
C7
F6
(G-7 C7)

(MED.)
NO MOE
- SONNY ROLLINS
Bb G-7b5 E°7 F7 Bb G-7b5
E°7 F7 Bb Bb/D Eb E°7
1. Bb/F
2. Bb/F F7 Bb
D7 G7 C7 F7
Bb G-7b5 E°7 F7 Bb G-7b5 E°7 F7
Bb Bb/D Eb E°7 Bb/F
SOLOS
Bb G-7 C-7 F7 Bb G-7 C-7 F7 Bb Bb/D Eb E°7 Bb/F C-7 F7 1. Bb F7 2. Bb
D7 G7 C7 F7
Bb G-7 C-7 F7 Bb G-7 C-7 F7 Bb Bb/D Eb E°7 Bb/F C-7 F7 Bb F7

NO SPLICE

(MED. UP)

—LEE KONITZ

G-7 | A-7b5 D7b9 | G-7

F-7 | Bb7 | Ebmaj7

A-7b5 | D7b9 | Eb7 D7b9

G-7 | Eb7 | Bb-7 Eb7 | Abmaj7

A-7b5 D7 | G-7 | A-7b5 D7b9 | G-7

F-7 | Bb7 | Ebmaj7

E07 | Bbmaj7/F

F#07 | G-7 | Eb7 | D7b9

G-7 | (A-7b5 D7b9)

294
NORTH ATLANTIC RUN
(MED. FAST LATIN)
– GERRY MULLIGAN
A
G6/9
D7sus4
1.
2.
G6/9
D7sus4
G6/9
D7sus4
B
Gmaj7
G6
A-7
D7
Gmaj7
G6
A-7
D7
Gmaj7
G6
C
1. A-7/D
B-7
Bb-6
A-7
Ab7b5
2. A-7/D
B-7
E-7
D-7
G7b5

C (SWING)
Cmaj7 C6 Cmaj7 C6 B-7 B-7/E E7b9
A-7 A-(maj7) A-7 D7 G G7#5
C C-6 B-7 E7b9
A-7 A-7/D D7 G C-7 F7
D (LATIN)
Bbmaj7 Bb6 Bbmaj7 Bb6 C-7 F7 C-7 F
Gmaj7 G6 Gmaj7 G6 A-7 D7
G G7 C C-(maj7)
B-7 Eb7/Bb A-7 D7sus4
E
F#7 G6/9 D7sus4
F#7 G6/9 D7sus4
FINE
SOLO ON B C D
AFTER SOLOS, D.S. AL FINE

(MED. SLOW BLUES)

NOW SEE HOW YOU ARE

– OSCAR PETTIFORD
WOODY HARRIS

(FAST LATIN)
NUTVILLE
—HORACE SILVER
INTRO
(BASS)
C-
(MELODY)
A
MELODY CAN BE HARMONIZED A 3RD AND/OR 4TH BELOW THROUGH A
C-9
BASS CONT. SIM.
F-7
Db9
C-9
Ab13
B
SWING
(Ab13)
G13
Gb13
F13
Ab13
BASS WALKS
G7#5
N.C.
C-9
(LATIN)
1.
2.
AFTER SOLDS, D.C. AL
(TAKE REPEAT)
NO ANTICIPATIONS ON SOLOS
3
C-9
Bb-9
Ab-9
G7#5
C-11

THE ODD COUPLE

— NEAL HEFTI

(MED.)

(MED. SWING)

OFF MINOR

-THELONIOUS MONK

OH, WHAT A BEAUTIFUL MORNIN'

(MED. FAST WALTZ)

-RICHARD RODGERS/OSCAR HAMMERSTEIN II

Ebmaj7 F-7/Bb Ebmaj7 F-7/Bb

Ebmaj7 F-7/Bb C-7 Db9

Ebmaj7 F-7 G-7 Abmaj7

G-7 C7b9 F-7 Bb7

Ebmaj7 Absus4 Ab

Ebmaj7 C-7 F-7 Bb7

Ebmaj7 Ab7b5 A°7

Eb/Bb Bb7 Eb6 (F-7/Bb)

(MED.)

OLD DEVIL MOON

BURTON LANE/
E.Y. HARBURG

ONE BY ONE

– WAYNE SHORTER

(Med. Swing)

One Foot in the Gutter

— Clark Terry

(MED. FAST)

ONE MORNING IN MAY

—HOAGY CARMICHAEL/
MITCHELL PARISH

Dmaj7
B7b9
E-7
A7
F#-7
B7b9
E-7
A7
Dmaj7
A-7
D7
Gmaj7
E-7b5
A7
D6
E-7
A7
D6
(E-7 A7)

(SLOW SWING)

OUT BACK OF THE BARN

-GERRY MULLIGAN

OYE COMO VA

(MED. LATIN)

-TITO PUENTE

INTRO

A-7 D9 A-7 D9

A- D A/E A- D A/E

A

A-7 D9 A-7 D9

B

A-7 D9 A-7 1. D9

2. D9 A-7 D9 A-7 D9

C

A-7 D9 A-7 D9

A- A-(maj7) D9sus4 D9 (PLAY 3x) A- A-(maj7) A-7 A-6

SOLOS

A-7 D9

AFTER SOLOS, D.S. AL ⊕ (TAKE REPEAT)

⊕

A- D A/E A- D A/E A-

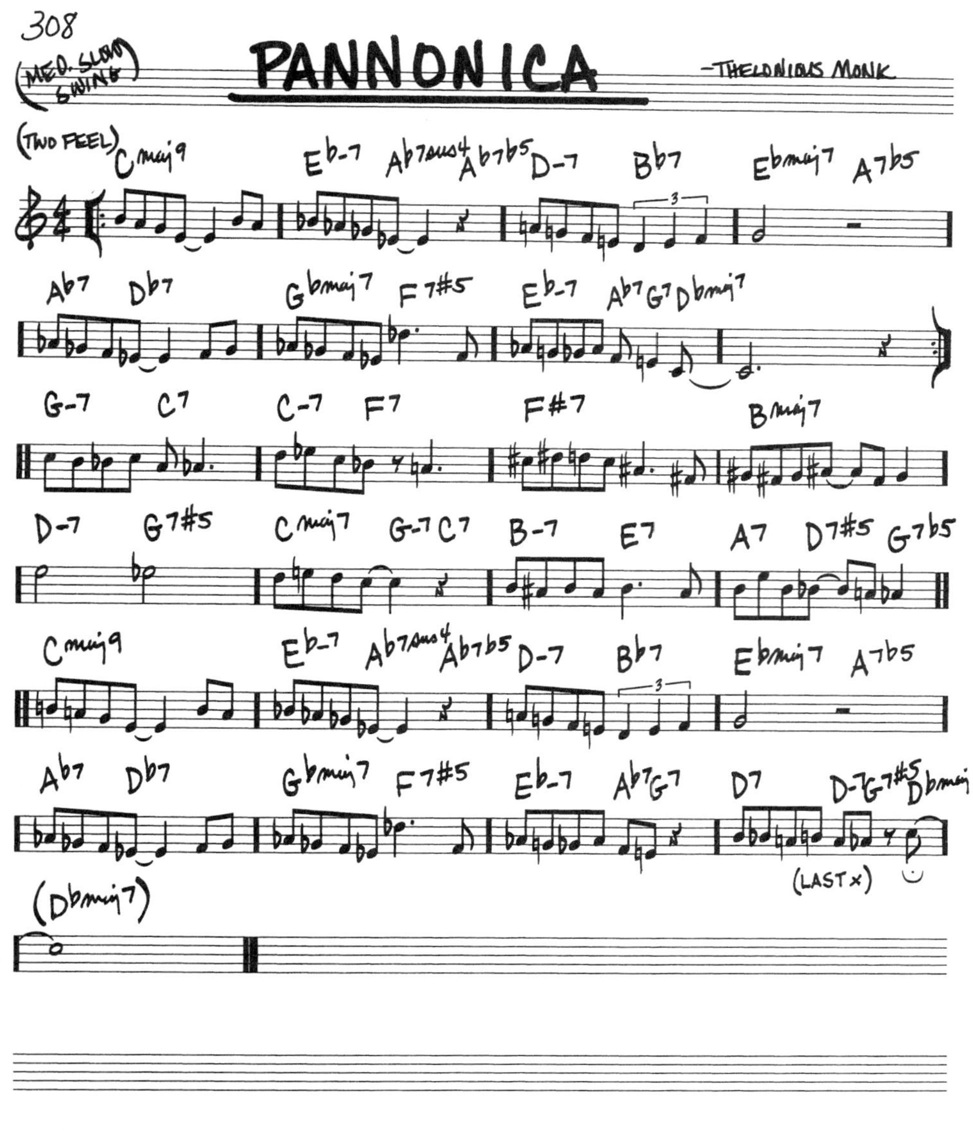
PANNONICA
– THELONIOUS MONK
(MED. SLOW SWING)
(TWO FEEL)
Cmaj9 Eb-7 Ab7sus4 Ab7b5 D-7 Bb7 Ebmaj7 A7b5
Ab7 Db7 Gbmaj7 F7#5 Eb-7 Ab7 G7 Dbmaj7
G-7 C7 C-7 F7 F#7 Bmaj7
D-7 G7#5 Cmaj7 G-7 C7 B-7 E7 A7 D7#5 G7b5
Cmaj9 Eb-7 Ab7sus4 Ab7b5 D-7 Bb7 Ebmaj7 A7b5
Ab7 Db7 Gbmaj7 F7#5 Eb-7 Ab7 G7 D7 D-7 G7#5 Dbmaj
(LAST x)
(Dbmaj7)

(UP)

PARISIAN THOROUGHFARE

-EARL "BUD" POWELL

PASSPORT

(BOP)

—CHARLIE PARKER

PEEL ME A GRAPE
-DAVE FRISHBERG
(MED. SLOW)
D-7
Eb7
D-7
Eb7
D-7
C7
Bb7
A7
D-7
Eb7
D-7
C-7 F7
Bb7
Bo7
F7#9
Bb7
Bo7
F7#9
Bb7
Bo7
F7#9
A7
N.C.
D-7
C7
1. Bb7 A7
2. Bb7 A7 D-7
A-7
D7
A-7
D7
G-
G-/F#
G-/F
C9/E
B-7
E7
B-7
E7
Bb7
A7
D-7
Eb7
D-7
Eb7
D-7
C7
Bb7
A7
D-7
Eb7
D-7
C-7 F7
Bb7
Bo7
F7#9
Bb7
Bo7
F7#9
Bb7
Bo7
F7#9
A7
N.C.
D-7
(C7
Bb7
A7)

(MED.)

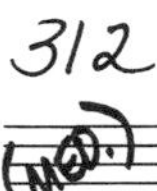

PENNIES FROM HEAVEN

-ARTHUR JOHNSTON/
JOHN BURKE

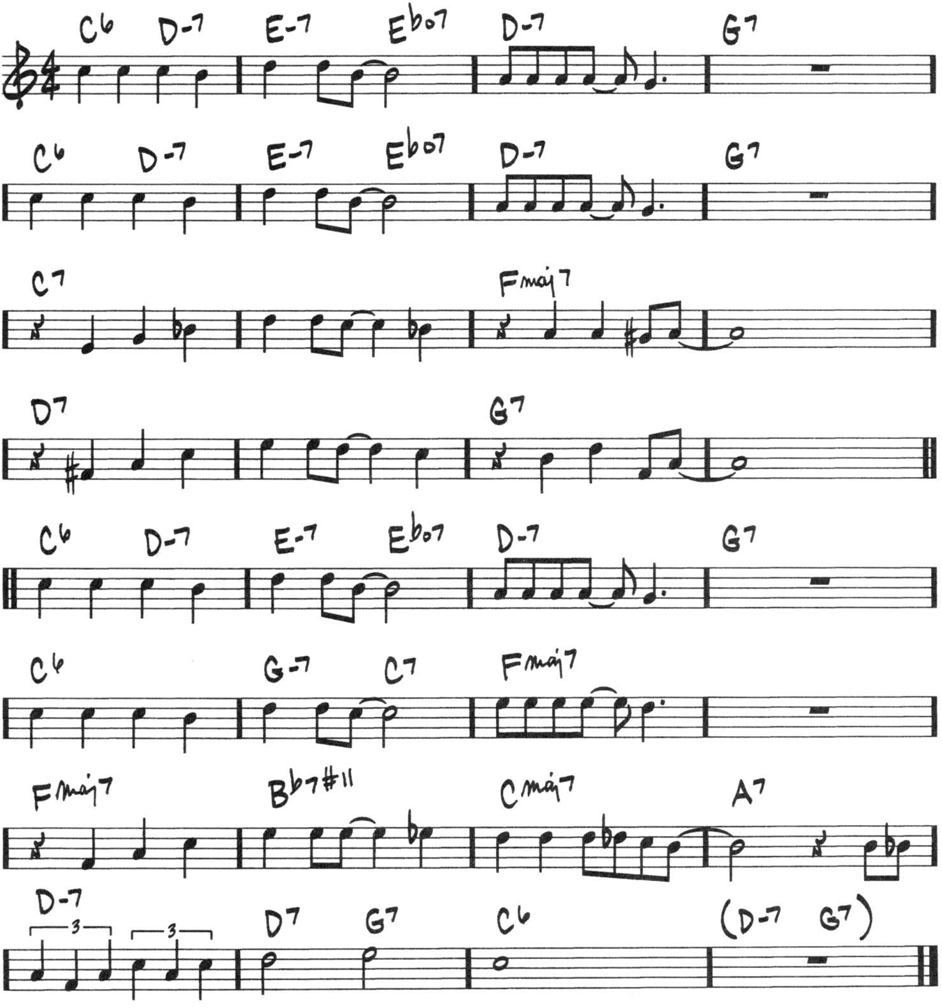
C6 D-7 E-7 Eb°7 D-7 G7
C6 D-7 E-7 Eb°7 D-7 G7
C7 Fmaj7
D7 G7
C6 D-7 E-7 Eb°7 D-7 G7
C6 G-7 C7 Fmaj7
Fmaj7 Bb7#11 Cmaj7 A7
D-7 3 3 D7 G7 C6 (D-7 G7)

(MED. SWING) PEOPLE WILL SAY WE'RE IN LOVE

—RICHARD RODGERS/OSCAR HAMMERSTEIN II

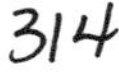

PERDIDO

(MED. SWING)

- JUAN TIZOL / HARRY LENK / ERVIN DRAKE

PETITE FLEUR
(LITTLE FLOWER)

-SIDNEY BECHET

UP (JAZZ/ROCK)
PETITS MACHINS
-MILES DAVIS/ GIL EVANS
HEAD
N.C.
C7#9
Db7#9
D7#9
Eb7#9
E7#9
Fmaj7
E7#9/F
Bb-7/F
D7#9/F
F-7
C7#9/E
SOLOS
REPEAT SOLOS TO END

(MAMBO)
PICADILLO (A LA PUENTE)
–TITO PUENTE
INTRO
(BASS)
A-7
A
A-7
B
A-7
C
A-7/E
D
SOLOS
OPEN SOLOS ON A-7
ON CUE:
E7
E
A-7
(PLAY 4x)
E7♯9
D.C. (INTRO) AL
(TAKE REPEAT)
A-11

PHASE DANCE
♩=176 (EVEN 8THS)
-PAT METHENY/ LYLE MAYS
INTRO
B-7
Bbmaj7
2
(MELODY)
A
B-7
RHYTHM CONT. SIM.
Bbmaj7
B-7
3
Bbmaj7
B HALF-TIME FEEL
Gmaj7/A

Gmaj13
END HALF-TIME FEEL
C
B-7
BASS PLAYS INTRO
B♭maj7
SOLO A B C
AFTER SOLOS, D.S. (PLAY PICKUPS)
VAMP INTRO TILL FADE

POINCIANA
(SONG OF THE TREE)
(MED. LATIN)
-NAT SIMON/
BUDDY BERNIER
INTRO
D13
A-7
D13
A-7
D13
D7
1. G6
2. G6
D13
A
Gmaj9
D-7
G7
C-7
Gmaj7
G6
A-7
D13
A
Gmaj9
D-7
G7

C-7
Gmaj7 G6
Gmaj7 G6
B
C-7
Dmaj7
D6
C-7
A-7
D13
A
Gmaj9
D-7
G7
C-7
Gmaj7
(A-7 D7)

(MED. BALLAD)

POLKA DOTS AND MOONBEAMS

-JIMMY VAN HEUSEN/JOHNNY BURKE

(MED.)

POOR BUTTERFLY

-RAYMOND HUBBELL/
JOHN L. GOLDEN

(BALLAD)

A PORTRAIT OF JENNY

-GORDON BURDGE/J. RUSSELL ROBINSON

Ebmaj7 Bb-7 Eb7 Abmaj7 Ab-7 Db7

1. G-7 C-7 F-7 Bb7 Ebmaj7 E°7 F-7 Bb7

2. G-7 C-7 F-7 Bb7 Eb6 A-7 D7

Gmaj7 C-7 F7 Bbmaj7 D-7b5 G7b9

C-7 F7 F-7 Bb7

Ebmaj7 Bb-7 Eb7 Abmaj7 Ab-7 Db7

G-7 C-7 F-7 Bb7 F-7 Bb7b9 Eb6 (F-7 Bb7)

(MED.)

PRISONER OF LOVE

— LEO ROBIN / CLARENCE GASKILL / RUSS COLUMBO

PURSUANCE
(PART III)

JOHN COLTRANE

(UP)

Bb-9

Ab-9

Bb-9

Gb9

F7#9

Bb-9

Bb-9

Ab-9

Bb-9

Gb9

F7#9

Bb-9

QUICKSILVER

- HORACE SILVER

(BOP)

(♩=160 JAZZ WALTZ)
QUESTION & ANSWER
-PAT METHENY
INTRO
D-
E-/A
D-
E-/A
(PLAY 4x)
A
D-
D-(#5)
D-6
D-7
G-7
A-7
Bbmaj7
C7sus4
D-
D-(#5)
D-6
C-7
F7
B7#9
Bb7b5
A7#9
D-
B
G-7/D
D7b9
G-/D
D7b9
G-7
Ab7
Dbmaj7
E7
Amaj7
C7
Fmaj7
A7b9

A
D-
D-(#5)
D-6
D-7
G-7
A-7
B♭maj7
C7sus4
D-
D-(#5)
D-6
C-7
F7
B7#9
B♭7♭5
A7#9
D-
G/A
SOLOS A A B A
AFTER SOLOS, D.S. AL
D-
E-/A
D-
E-/A
REPEAT AS DESIRED

(MAMBO)
RAN KAN KAN
-TITO PUENTE
INTRO
D
C
D
C
BASS DOUBLES MELODY
D
N.C.
D
N.C.
A
D
A-7
1.
2.
B
(LAST X)
C SOLOS
D
ON CUE:
BACK TO C FOR ADDITIONAL SOLOS
AFTER SOLOS, D.S. AL (TAKE REPEATS)

(MED. SWING)

RE: PERSON I KNEW

-BILL EVANS

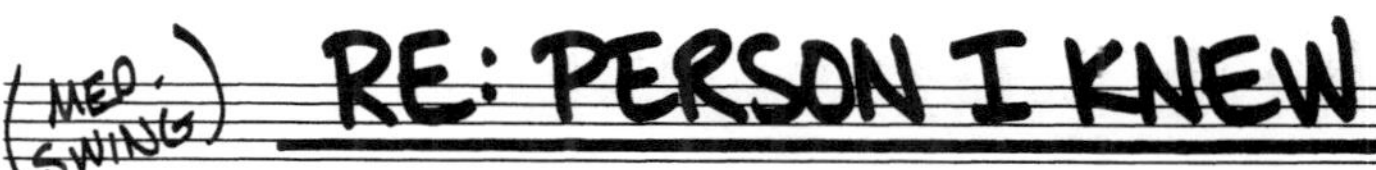

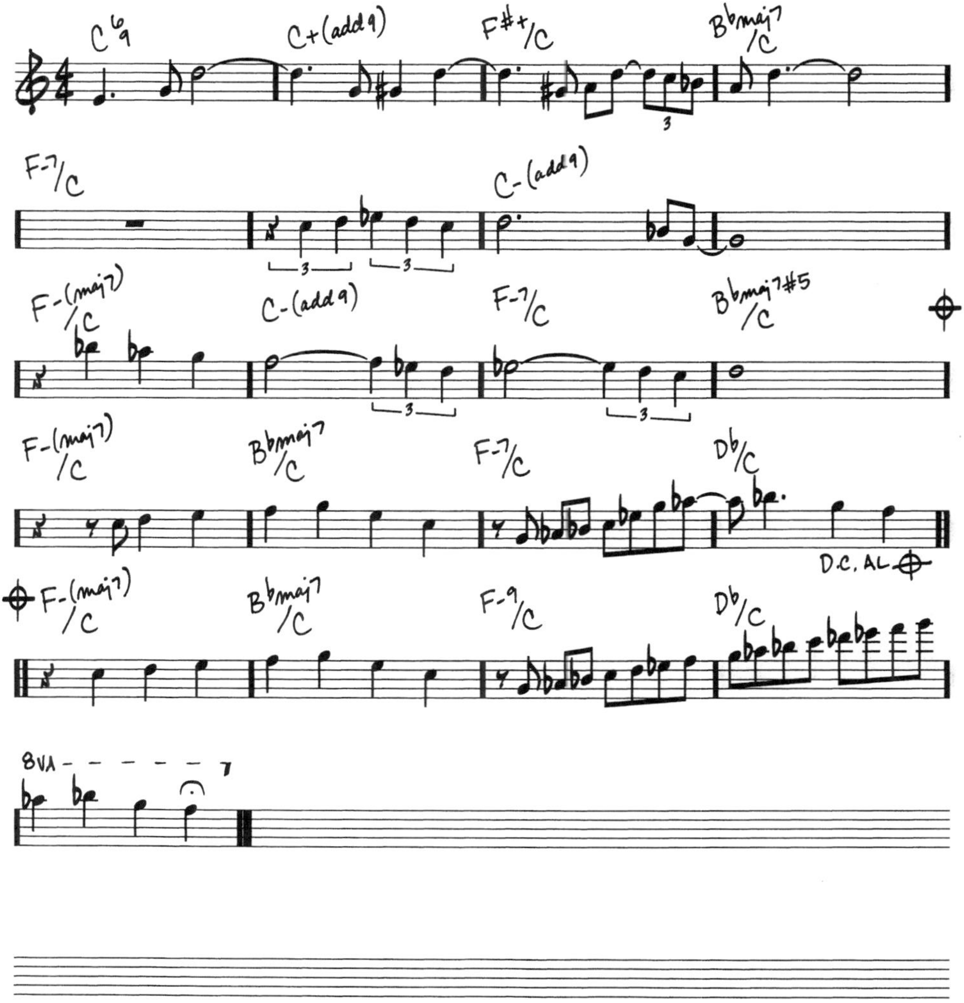
C6/9
C+(add 9)
F#+/C
Bbmaj7/C
F-7/C
C-(add 9)
F-(maj7)/C
C-(add 9)
F-7/C
Bbmaj7#5/C
F-(maj7)/C
Bbmaj7/C
F-7/C
Db/C
D.C. AL
F-(maj7)/C
Bbmaj7/C
F-9/C
Db/C
8VA

THE RED ONE

(FAST REGGAE EVEN 8THS)

-PAT METHENY

REVELATION

- KENNY BARRON

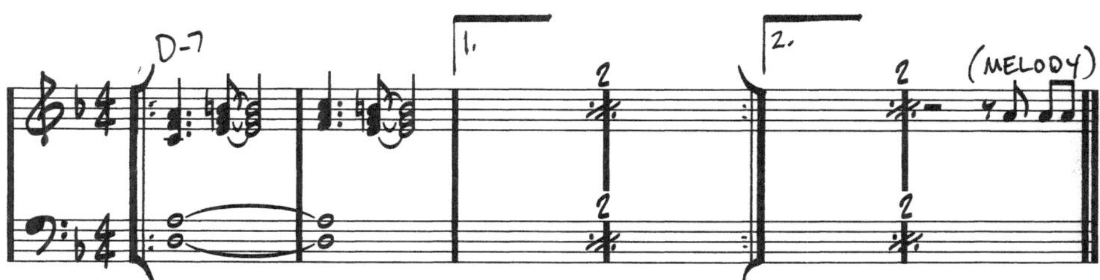

RHYTHM-A-NING
THELONIOUS MONK
(MED. SWING)
A (BASS DOUBLES MELODY)
Bb
(WALK)
Eb
Bb
1.
2.
B (BASS CONT. WALK)
D7
G7
C7
F7
C (BASS DOUBLES MELODY)
Bb
(WALK)
Eb
Bb
SOLOS (RHYTHM CHANGES)
(LAST X)
Bb G7 C-7 F7 Bb G7 C-7 F7 Bb Bb7
Eb E°7 1. Bb/F F7 Bb F7 2. Bb/F F7 Bb
D7 G7 C7 F7
Bb G7 C-7 F7 Bb G7 C-7 F7 Bb Bb7 Eb E°7 Bb/F F7 Bb F7

RIGHT AS RAIN

(BALLAD)

HAROLD ARLEN/
E.Y. HARBURG

ROOM 608

— Horace Silver

(Med. Up)

INTRO

C-7/F D-7/F C-7/F F7#11#9

D7#11#9 Db7#11#9 C7#11#9 F6 N.C. F7#9#5

HEAD

Bbmaj7 G7 C-7 F7 Bbmaj7 G7 C-7 F7

F-7 Bb7 Eb6 E°7 1. Bb/F G7 C-7 F7

2. Bb/F G7 C-7 F7 Bb6 F-7b5 Bb7#9(#5)

Ebmaj7 Ab-7b5 Db7#9(#5)

Gbmaj7 F7#9 Bbmaj7 G7 C-7 F7

Bbmaj7 G7 C-7 F7 F-7 Bb7 Eb6 E°7

Bb/F G7 C-7 F7 Bb6

ROSE ROOM

(MED. SWING)

–ART HICKMAN/
HARRY WILLIAMS

ROSEWOOD
-WOODY SHAW
MED. (EVEN 8ths)
INTRO
A-7 Amaj7
Bbmaj7/A Bbmaj7 Abmaj7 G-7 Abmaj7
A
G-7 F-7 G-7 F-7 C-7 Bb-7 Gbmaj7
G-7 F-7 G-7 F-7 C-7 Bb-7 Gbmaj7
Abmaj7 Ab-7 Db7
3
Gbmaj7 B7 E7
C-7 Bb-7 C-7 Bb-7 Gbmaj7 Emaj7 Dmaj7#11

C-7
Bb-7
C-7
Bb-7
Gbmaj7
Emaj7
Dmaj7#11
1.
B
B7sus4
A7sus4
B7sus4
A7sus4
G-7
F-7
G-7
F-7
Bb7sus4
A-7
Amaj7
Bbmaj7
/A
Bbmaj7
Abmaj7
G-7
Abmaj7
2.
C
Bb7sus4
Gbmaj7
G-7
Ab7sus4
Bb7sus4
Gbmaj7
G-7
Ab7sus4
Bb7sus4
Gbmaj7
Ab/G
Ab7sus4
FINE
SOLO A B A C
AFTER SOLOS, D.C. AL FINE
(TAKE REPEAT)

ROUND TRIP

—ORNETTE COLEMAN

(MED FAST)

[OPEN SOLOS ON E♭]

RUBBERNECK

– FRANK ROSOLINO

(MED. BLUES)
SACK OF WOE
-JULIAN ADDERLEY
INTRO
(EVEN 8THS)
F5
(PIANO)
A
F5
CONT. RHYTHM SIM.
Bb5
F5
C5
Bb5
F5
B
(SWING)
F6
F7
Bb7
F7
G-7
C7
F6 N.C.
F5
W/ INTRO RHYTHM
[SOLO ON F BLUES]

ST. THOMAS

(CALYPSO)

– SONNY ROLLINS

(UP)

SALT PEANUTS

—John "Dizzy" Gillespie/
Kenny Clarke

F F/A Bb Bo7 F/C N.C.

F F/A Bb Bo7 F/C N.C. 1. 2.

A7 D7

G7 C7

F F/A Bb Bo7 F/C N.C.

F F/A Bb Bo7 F/C N.C.

SOLOS

F G-7 C7 F G-7 C7 F7 Bb7 Bb-7 F 1. G-7 C7 2.

A7 D7 G7 C7

F G-7 C7 F G-7 C7 F7 Bb7 Bb-7 F G-7 C7

SANDU
(MED. BLUES)
-CLIFFORD BROWN
Eb7
Ab7
Eb7
Ab7
Eb7
Bb PEDAL
Eb
1.
F-7
E7#11 #9
2. N.C.
N.C.
(SOLO BREAK)
3
SOLOS
Eb7
Ab7
Eb7
Ab7
Eb7
G-7
C7
F-7
Bb7
Eb7
(C-7
F-7
Bb7)
Bb PEDAL
Eb9#11
AFTER SOLOS, D.S. AL
TAKE REPEAT

Say It
(Over and Over Again)

– Frank Loesser/
Jimmy McHugh

SEGMENT

(MED. BOP)

– CHARLIE PARKER

(JAZZ WALTZ)

SERENADE TO A SOUL SISTER

—HORACE SILVER

SERENE

-Eric Dolphy

(MED. SLOW SWING)

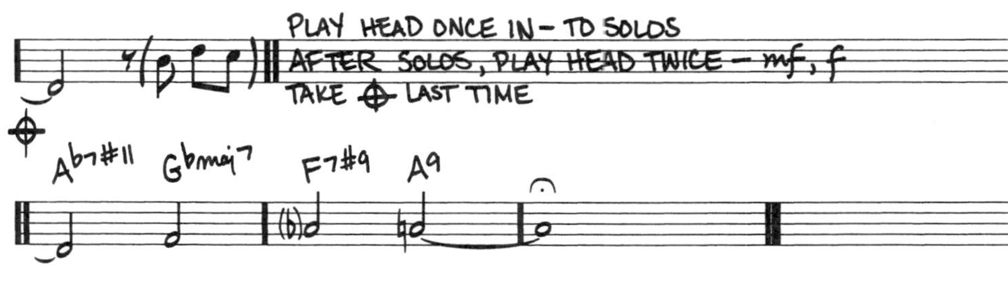

SHUTTERBUG

(UP)

—J.J. JOHNSON

G-7

C-7

G-7

Bb-7 Eb7 A-7 D7#5(b9) G-7

(MED.)
SILVER'S SERENADE
-HORACE SILVER
E-9
Bb-9
A-9
Eb-9
A-7
C-7
B7
Bbmaj7
C-7
D-7
Ebmaj7
A-7
1. D7b5
2. D7b5
AFTER SOLOS, D.C. AL
(TAKE REPEAT)
D7b5
G6/9
(FREELY)
Gmaj7#11

♩=128 (JAZZ WALTZ)

SIMONE

–FRANK FOSTER

(MED.)

SING, YOU SINNERS

—SAM COSLOW / W. FRANKE HARLING

(BALLAD) SMOKE GETS IN YOUR EYES

—JEROME KERN/
OTTO HARBACH

(SAMBA)
SÓ DANÇO SAMBA
(JAZZ 'N' SAMBA)
-ANTONIO CARLOS JOBIM/
VINICIUS DE MORAES/
NORMAN GIMBEL
C6
A7#5
D9
D-9
G7
C6
1.
G9sus4
2.
G-7
C7
F6
A-7
D7
D-7
G7
C6
A7#5
D9
D-9
G7
C6
(D-7
G7#5)

SMOKE RINGS

– H. Eugene Gifford/
Ned Washington

(MED. SLOW)

Fmaj7
C7#5
Fmaj7
C-7
F7
Bbmaj7
G-7b5
C7
F6
D-7
G-7
C7
Fmaj7
C7#5
Bb7
A7#5
D-7
G7
Bbmaj7
G-7b5
C7
3
F6
(G-7
C7)

SOFTLY AS IN A MORNING SUNRISE

(MED.)

–SIGMUND ROMBERG/OSCAR HAMMERSTEIN II

(UP)

SOME OTHER BLUES

—JOHN COLTRANE

(MED.)

SOMEBODY LOVES YOU

- PETER DE ROSE / CHARLIE TOBIAS

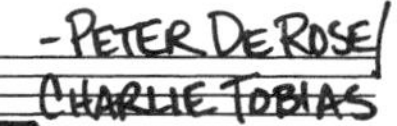

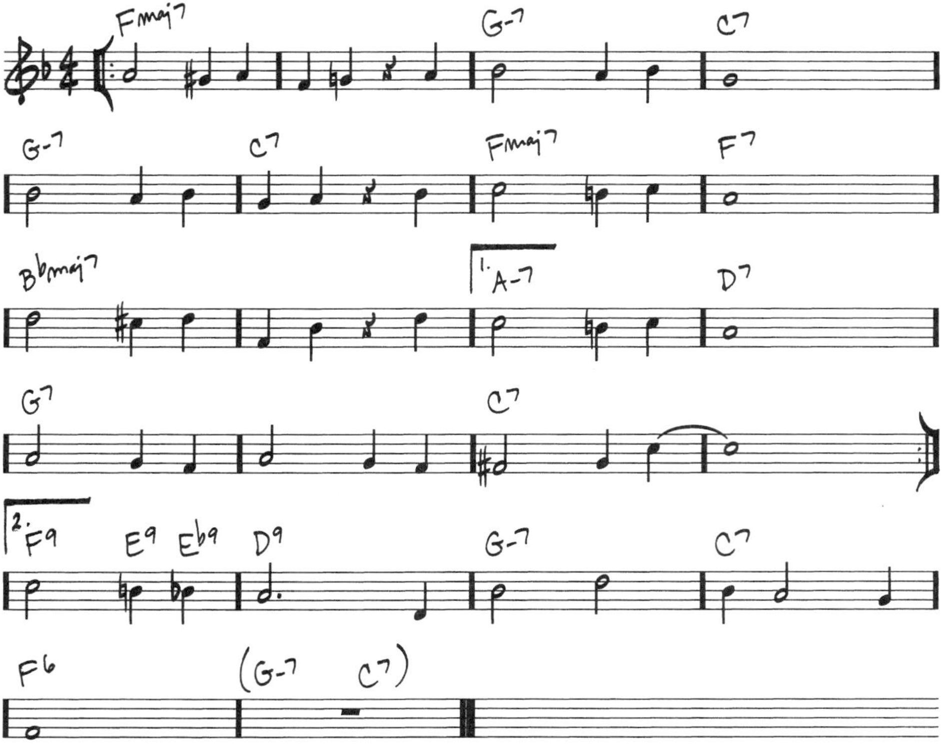

Fmaj7
G-7
C7
G-7
C7
Fmaj7
F7
B♭maj7
1.
A-7
D7
G7
C7
2.
F9
E9
E♭9
D9
G-7
C7
F6
(G-7 C7)

SOMETHING WONDERFUL

(BALLAD)

- RICHARD RODGERS / OSCAR HAMMERSTEIN II

Gmaj7 G9 Cmaj7 F° Gmaj7 G9

Cmaj7 F9 Gmaj7 Cmaj7

1. A-7 D7sus4 D7 2. A7 D7sus4 D7

G-7 D-7 G-7 A7 Dmaj7

G-7 G-7/F E-7b5 A7b9 Dmaj7 A-7 D7

Gmaj7 G9 Cmaj7 F9 Gmaj7 G9 Cmaj7 F9

Gmaj7 Cmaj7 A7 D7sus4 D7

B7 E-7 G7 C6 F9

Gmaj7 G9 Cmaj7 F9 B-7 E7 A-7 D7sus4

G6 (A-7 D7)

SONG FOR BILBAO
- PAT METHENY
(LATIN EVEN 8ths ♩=180)
C7sus4 C6 C7sus4
C6 C7sus4
(MELODY ENTERS 2nd X)
Gbmaj7b5 Ab/Db Gbmaj7b5
C7sus4 C6 C7sus4
F Bb Eb F Db Eb F G
C7sus4 C6 C7sus4
C6 C7sus4
(BASS & RHYTHM AS BEFORE)
Gbmaj7b5 Ab/Db Gbmaj7b5
C7sus4 C6 C7sus4
AFTER SOLOS, D.C. AL ⊕
(NO REPEAT) (PLAY PICKUPS)
Gbmaj7b5
C7sus4
(W/ FILLS)

(MED. SWING)

SONG FOR STRAYHORN

-GERRY MULLIGAN

Dmaj7 E-7/D Dmaj7 E-7/D
Dmaj7 A-7 Dmaj7 1. A7sus4 2. Ab7b9(#11)
Gmaj7 Gmaj7#11 F#-7 Fmaj7#11
E-7 Fmaj7 F#-7 B7 Emaj7 Bb7(#11)
A7sus4 A7 Dmaj7 E-7/D
Dmaj7 E-7/D Dmaj7 A-7
Dmaj7 A-7 Dmaj7 (E-7/D)

SONGBIRD
(THANK YOU FOR YOUR LOVELY SONG)
(BALLAD)
- LOONIS McGLOHON
D7#9 Ebmaj7 Bb-7 Eb7 Abmaj7 F-7 D-7 G7
C-7 F7 D-7 G-7 Eb-7 Ab7 1. C-7 F7 F-7 Bb7
2. Dbmaj7 B7b5 Bb7 Eb-7 Ab7 F-7 Bb-7 G-7 C7
C-7 Bo7 Bb7sus4 Bb7b5 D7#9 Ebmaj7 Bb-7 Eb7 Abmaj7 F-7
D-7 G7 C-7 Bb-7 Eb7 Abmaj7 Ab-7 G-7 C-7 F-7 Bb7
Eb6

S.O.S.

-John L. (Wes) Montgomery

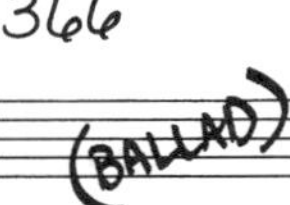

SOUL EYES

—MAL WALDRON

(MED. LATIN)

SPEAK LIKE A CHILD

–HERBIE HANCOCK

Db7#9 Ab7#9 E7sus4 A-7

Bb7 Bb-7 Eb7

Ab7sus4 Ab7sus4(b9) G7#9

Gbmaj7#11 Gbo7 1. Eb7sus4

Eb7 Eb-7 D7#9 G-7 C7 Fmaj7 Bb-7

A-7 E7sus4 A-7 E7sus4 A-7

E7sus4 2. Dbmaj7b5/F Gbmaj7#11

Cmaj7/C# Bbmaj7/C Cmaj7/B Bb-7 A-7 E7sus4 A-7 E7sus4

SOLO

A-7 E7sus4 A-7 E7sus4

VAMP

AFTER SOLOS, D.C. (TAKE REPEAT)
FADE OUT OVER VAMP

(MED.)
SPIRAL
-JOHN COLTRANE
G/D
Gb/D
F/D
E/D
Eb/D
D
G-
C7
B-
C#-7b5
F#7b9
B-
E-
A7
G7
B-
E-7
A7
Dmaj7
E-7
Fmaj7
A7
G/D
Gb/D
F/D
E/D
Eb/D
D
G-
C7
B-
C#-7b5
F#7b9
B-
(C#-7b5
F#7b9)

SPRING WILL BE A LITTLE LATE THIS YEAR

(BALLAD)

-FRANK LOESSER

(MED. BLUES)

SQUEEZE ME

—CLARENCE WILLIAMS/
THOMAS "FATS" WALLER

(MED. SWING)

STABLEMATES

-BENNY GOLSON

STORMY WEATHER
(KEEPS RAININ' ALL THE TIME)
(BALLAD)
- HAROLD ARLEN/
TED KOEHLER
Gmaj7 E7b9 A-7 D7 B-7 E7b9
A-7 D9 G6 E7b9 A-7 D7#5(b9)
1. G6 E-7 A-7 D7b9 2. G6 D-7 G7b9
C6 C#o7 G6/D G7 C6 C#o7 G6/D G7
3
C6 C#o7 G6/D G6 B-7 E-7 Eb9#11 D9
Gmaj7 E7b9 A-7 D7 B-7 E7b9 A-7 D9
G6 E7b9 A-7 D7#5(b9) G6 (E-7 A-7 D7b9)

STRAIGHT LIFE

– FREDDIE HUBBARD

(MED. EVEN 8ths)

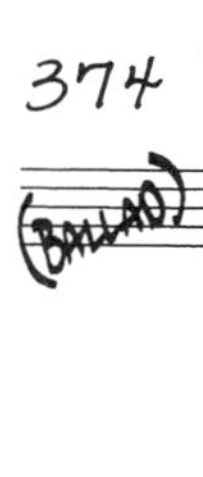

STRAYHORN 2

(BALLAD)

– GERRY MULLIGAN

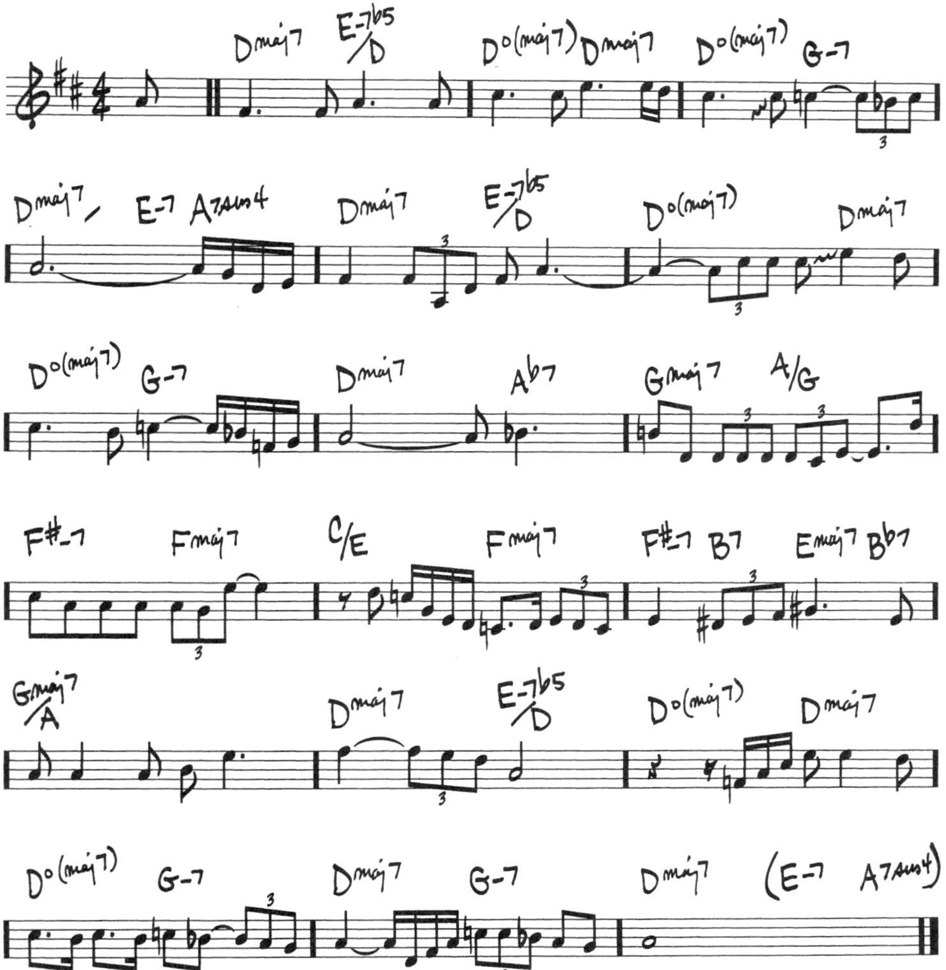
Dmaj7 E-7b5/D D°(maj7) Dmaj7 D°(maj7) G-7
Dmaj7 / E-7 A7sus4 Dmaj7 E-7b5/D D°(maj7) Dmaj7
D°(maj7) G-7 Dmaj7 Ab7 Gmaj7 A/G
F#-7 Fmaj7 C/E Fmaj7 F#-7 B7 Emaj7 Bb7
Gmaj7/A Dmaj7 E-7b5/D D°(maj7) Dmaj7
D°(maj7) G-7 Dmaj7 G-7 Dmaj7 (E-7 A7sus4)

STRODE RODE

—SONNY ROLLINS

STROLLIN'

— HORACE SILVER

(TWO FEEL)

Dbmaj7 | | E-7 A7 | Eb-7 Ab7 |

Dbmaj7 | | Ab-7 Db7 | G-7 C7 |

1. F-7 | Bb7#9 | Eb-7 | Ab13 Ab7#5 |

Dbmaj7 | Bb-7 | Eb7#11 | D7#9 :|

2. F-7 | Bb-7 | Eb7#11 | F#-7 B7 |

F-7 Bb7 | Eb-7 Ab7 | ⊕ Db6 F-7 | Eb-7 Ab7 ||

BASS WALKS ON SOLOS
AFTER SOLOS, D.C. AL ⊕
(TAKE REPEAT)

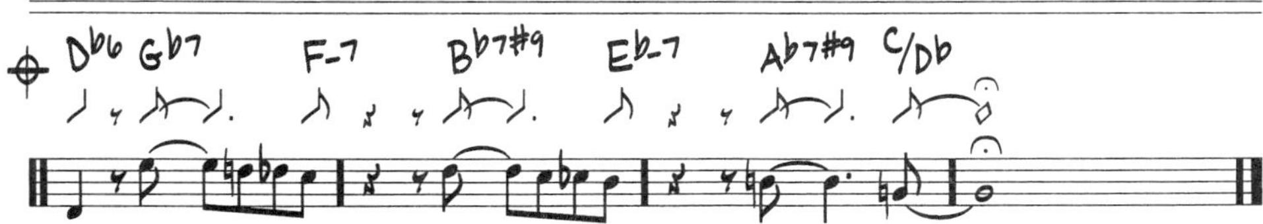

(MED. SWING)
STRUTTIN' WITH SOME BARBECUE
- LILLIAN HARDIN ARMSTRONG / DON RAYE
Fmaj7
F6
Fmaj7
D7
G-7
C7
C#o7
D-7
G7
C7
Fmaj7
F6
C-7
F7
Bb6
Bb-6
Fmaj7
D7
G-7
C7
F6
(Db7
C7)

SUBCONSCIOUS LEE

(MED. UP)

— LEE KONITZ

SUDDENLY IT'S SPRING

—JAMES VAN HEUSEN/
JOHNNY BURKE

(MED.)

SUMMER IN CENTRAL PARK

(JAZZ WALTZ)

-HORACE SILVER

Fmaj7 A7#5 D-7 G7

Dbmaj7 Gbmaj7 G-7 A7b9

Dmaj7 D-7

Dmaj7 D-7

Dmaj7 D-7

Dmaj7 G-7 C7b9

Fmaj7 A7#5 D-7 G7

Dbmaj7 Gbmaj7 Amaj7 Dmaj7

Dbmaj7 G-7 C7b9

Abmaj7 Gbmaj7b5 Fmaj7 G-7 C7b9

AFTER SOLOS, D.C. AL

G-7 C7b9 Abmaj7 Gbmaj7b5 Fmaj7

S'POSIN'
(MED.)
-ANDY RAZAF/
PAUL DENNIKER
Bbmaj7
C-7
F7
Bbmaj7
C-7
F7
Bbmaj7
A-7b5
D7#9
G-7
C7
C-7
F7
Bbmaj7
C-7
F7
Bbmaj7
F-7
Bb7
Eb6
Ab7
G-7
E-7b5
Eb7
D7
G-7
Bbmaj7
G7#9
C-7
F7
Bb6
(C-7 F7)

SWEET AND LOVELY
(BALLAD)
-GUS ARNHEIM/ CHARLES N. DANIELS/ HARRY TOBIAS
G-7 C7 G-7 C7
F7 Bbmaj7 Eb9 Cmaj7 G7 C6
F-7 Bb7 Cmaj7 F-7 Bb7 Cmaj7
Ab-7 Db7 Ebmaj7 Ab7 G7
G-7 C7 G-7 C7
F7 Bbmaj7 Eb9 Cmaj7 G7 C6

(MED. FAST)

THE SWEETEST SOUNDS

—RICHARD RODGERS

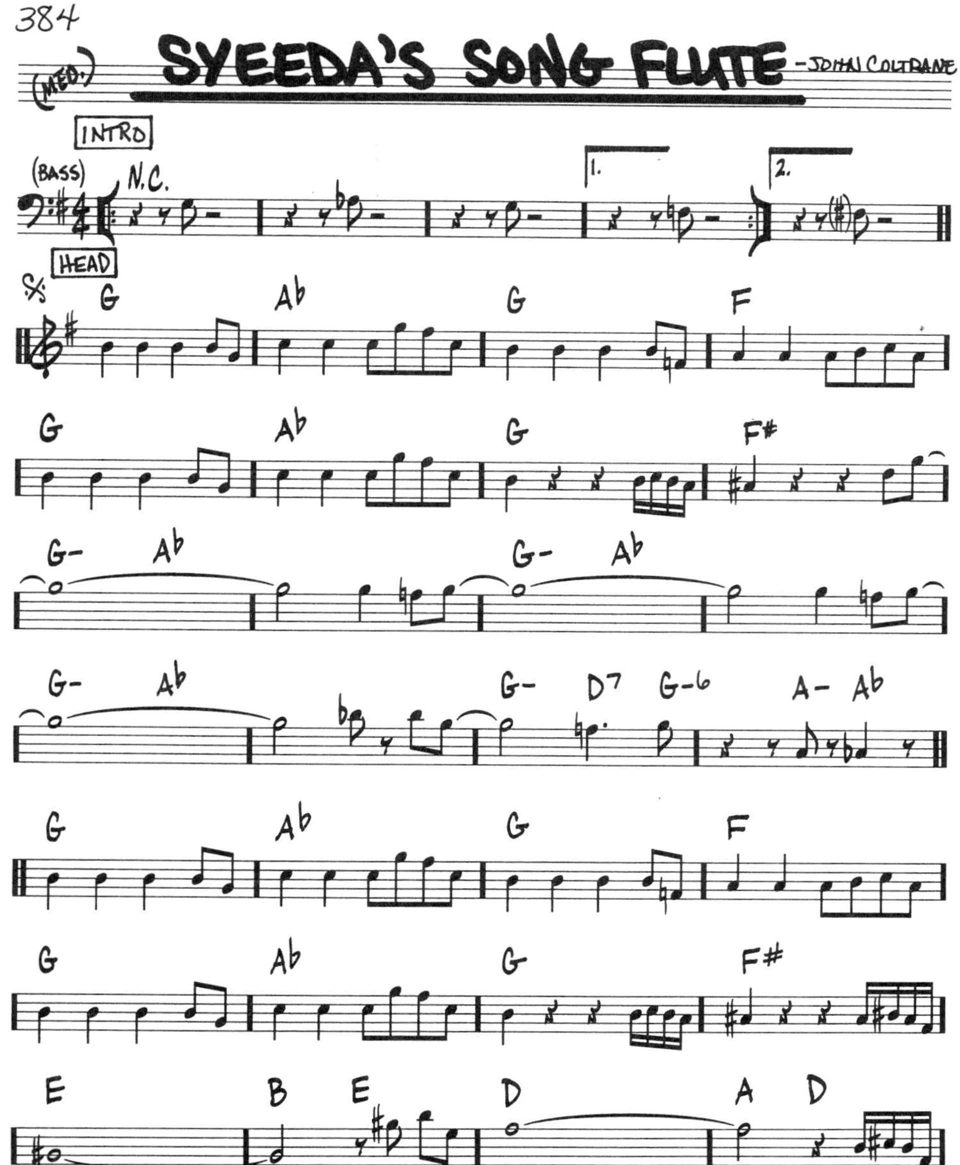
SYEEDA'S SONG FLUTE
- JOHN COLTRANE
(MED.)
INTRO
(BASS)
N.C.
1.
2.
HEAD
G Ab G F
G Ab G F#
G- Ab G- Ab
G- Ab G- D7 G-6 A- Ab
G Ab G F
G Ab G F#
E B E D A D

G
B
E
F#
C#
F#
FINE
SOLOS
G
Ab7
G
Ab7
G
Ab7
G
F#7
G-
Ab
G-
Ab
G-
Ab
G-
Ab
G
Ab7
G
Ab7
G
Ab7
G
F#7
E7
D7
E7
F#7
AFTER SOLOS, D.S. AL FINE

'TAIN'T WHAT YOU DO (IT'S THE WAY THAT CHA DO IT)

(MED.)

-SY OLIVER/
JAMES YOUNG

Take Ten

(Med. Swing)

— Paul Desmond

(MED. UP LATIN)
TANGA
-JOHN "DIZZY" GILLESPIE
INTRO
N.C.
(2nd x)
A
Fmaj7
Bb7
Fmaj7
A-7
D7#5
G-7
Eb7
G-7
C7sus4
1.
F6
C7
2.
F6
B
Bb-7
Eb7

Ab6
F7#5
Bb-7
Eb7
Ab6
A-7
D7
G6
E7#5
A-7
D7
G7
C7
D.S. AL ⊕ (HEAD IN/OUT)
C7sus4
N.C.
FINE
SOLO A A B A (NO ⊕)
AFTER SOLOS, D.S. AL ⊕
(PLAY PICKUP, TAKE REPEATS)

TANGERINE

(MED.)

—VICTOR SCHERTZINGER/
JOHNNY MERCER

A TASTE OF HONEY

- BOBBY SCOTT / RIC MARLOW

TEEN TOWN

-JACO PASTORIUS

(MED. FUNK)

D7
C7
A7
F7
D7
C7
A7
F7
D7
C7
A7
F7
D7
B7
E7
C#7
A7
F#7
(PLAY 5x)
(BASS FIGURE 1st AND 2nd TIME ONLY)
E7
C#7
A7
F#7
E7
C#7
A7
F#7
E7
C#7
A7
F#7
E7
(E7)
E7#9
F#/A# E7/D G6

(MED. SWING)

TEENIE'S BLUES

-OLIVER E. NELSON

TELEPHONE SONG

(MED. BOSSA)

-ROBERTO MENESCAL/NORMAN GIMBEL/RONALDO BOSCOLI

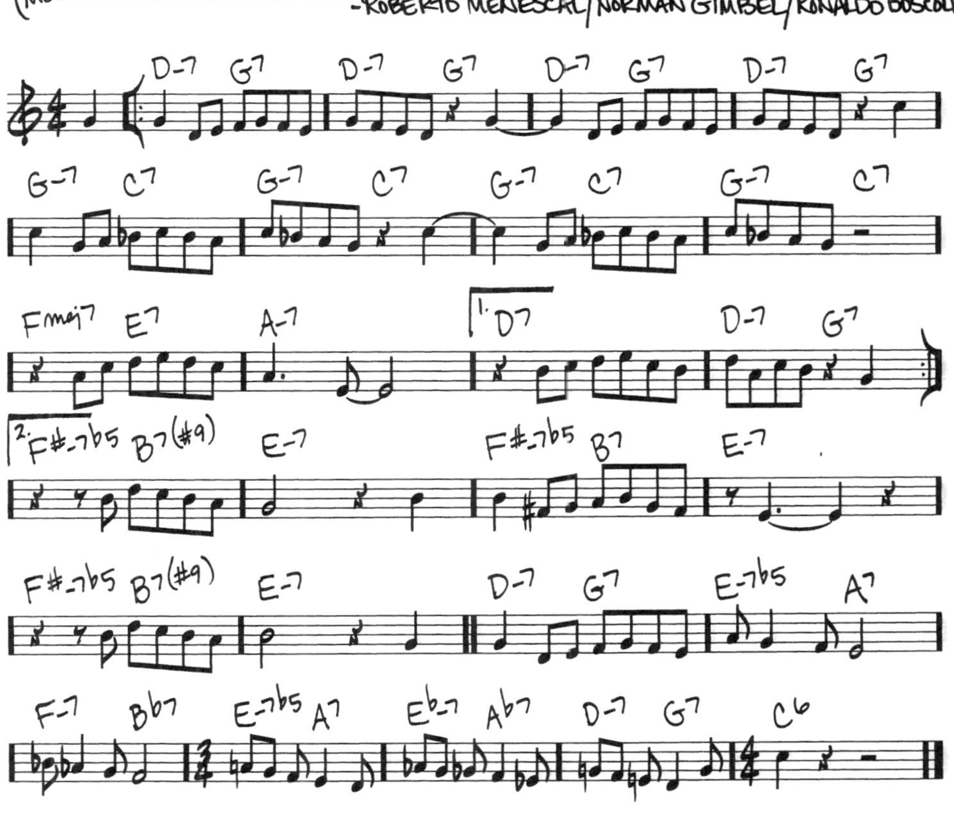

(FAST BOP)

TEMPUS FUGIT

— EARL BUD POWELL

(MED. SWING)

(LOVE IS) THE TENDER TRAP

–JAMES VAN HEUSEN / SAMMY CAHN

F6 F#o7 C-7/G C7

C-7 F7 Bbmaj7 A7#5 D7 C/E D-7/F D7/F# G7

G-7 C7sus4 1. F6 D-7 G-7 C7 2. F6

E-7b5 A7 D-7

E-7b5 A7 D-7 G7 G-7 C7#5

F6 F#o7 C-7/G C7

C-7 F7 Bbmaj7 A7#5 D7 C/E D-7/F D7/F#

G7 G-7 C7sus4 A-7b5 D7

G-7 C7 F6 (D-7 G-7 C7)

TENOR MADNESS

(MED. UP)

—SONNY ROLLINS

(BALLAD)

THERE ARE SUCH THINGS

-STANLEY ADAMS/ABEL BAER/GEORGE W. MEYER

Cmaj7 G-7 C7#5 F6 G7#5

D-7 G7#5 Cmaj7 E-7 A7

D-7 Ebo7 E-7 A7

D-7 D7 D-7 G7 D-7/G

Cmaj7 G-7 C7#5 F6 G7#5

D-7 B7 E7sus4 E-7b5 A7

D-7 F-6 Cmaj7 E-7 A7

D7 G7 C6 (D-7 G7)

THERE'S A SMALL HOTEL

(MED.)

—RICHARD RODGERS/LORENZ HART

THESE FOOLISH THINGS (REMIND ME OF YOU)

(MED. BALLAD)

JACK STRACHEY/ HOLT MARVELL

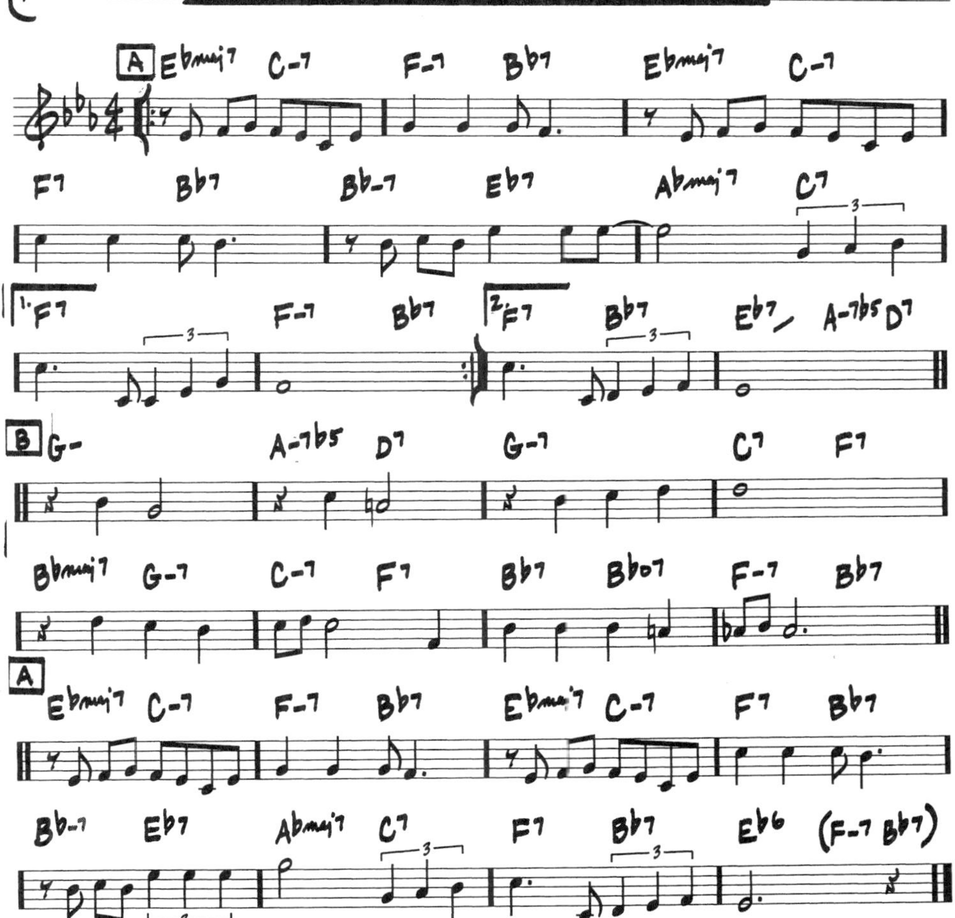

(UP)

THINGS TO COME

– DIZZY GILLESPIE/
GIL FULLER

(MED. LATIN ROCK EVEN 8THS)
THIS MASQUERADE
-LEON RUSSELL
INTRO
F-7
(SOLO)
Bb7
REPEAT AS DESIRED
A
F-
F-(maj7)
F-7
Bb7
F-7
Db7
G-7
C7#5
F-
F-(maj7)
F-7
Bb7
Db7
C7#5
F-7
E-7 A7
B
Eb-7
Ab7
Dbmaj7
Bb7#5
Eb-7
Ab7
Dbmaj7
D-7
G13
G7#5
Cmaj7
G-7
G13
G7#5
G-7/C
Gb13
D.S. AL
C7#5
F-7
Bb7
[SOLO ON INTRO]

THREE BASE HIT
(BRIGHT)
—PAT MARTINO
A-7
B-7b5
E7#9
Bb7b5
Ab-7
Db9#11
F#-7
B7
E-7
A7
Dmaj7
Gmaj7
G7#5
C9#11
(SOLO)
Db7#9
F#7sus4
Gmaj13
FILL
SOLOS
G7

(BALLAD)

THE THRILL IS GONE

–RAY HENDERSON/
LEW BROWN

THE THUMPER

(MED. FAST BLUES)

—JIMMY HEATH

(BALLAD)

TILL THERE WAS YOU

– MEREDITH WILLSON

TIPPIN'
(MED. UP SWING)
– HORACE SILVER
Bb6 G7b9 C-7 C#o7 Bb/D G7b9 C-7 F7
Bb7 Eb6 Eo7 Bb/F G7b9 C7 F7
Eb6 Eo7 Bb/F G-7 C-7 F7 Bb6 A-7
D7 Ab-7 Db7 G-7
C7 C-7b5 F7 Bb6 G7b9
C-7 C#o7 Bb/D G7b9 C-7 F7 Bb7
Eb6 Eo7 Bb/F G-7 C-7 F7 Bb6

TOMORROW'S DESTINY

- WOODY SHAW

(BALLAD)

TOO YOUNG

- SID LIPPMAN/SYLVIA DEE

Bb6 | D-7 | G-7 | C-7 F7

Bb6 | D-7 | Ebmaj7 | D-7b5 G7

C-7 C-7/Bb | A-7b5 D7b9 | G-7 | D-7 Db7

C-7 | F7 | D-7 G7 | C-7 F7

Bb6 | D-7 | G-7 | C-7 F7

Bb6 | Bb7 | Eb6 | D-7b5 G7

C-7 | Eb- | D-7 | G7

C-7 | F7 | Bb6 | (C-7 F7)

(MED. SWING)

THE TOUCH OF YOUR LIPS

– RAY NOBLE

TRANE'S BLUES

(MED. BLUES)

—JOHN COLTRANE

TURNAROUND

(MED. BLUES)

– ORNETTE COLEMAN

[SOLOS ON C BLUES]

TRICK
(MED. SWING)
-PATRICK AZZARA
INTRO
A-7 D6 A-7 D6 A-7 D6 A-7 D6
A
A-7 G6 Gb6 F13 A-7 G6
E-7 A7b9 D6 Bb/Db C6 Ab/B
B-7b5 E7#9 1. A-7 F#o7 B-7b5 E7#9
A-7 D6 A-7 D6 2. A-7 F#o7
B-7b5 E7#9 A-7 D6 A-7 D6
B
D-7 G7 E-7 A7b5 D-7b5 G7b5
C7#9 B-7b5 E7#9 C#-7b5 F#7#9 D-7b5 G7b5

C7#9
A
A-7
G6
Gb6
F13
3
A-7
G6
E-7
A7b9
D6
Bb/Db
3
C6
Ab/B
B-7b5
E7#9
A-7
F#o7
B-7b5
E7#9
A-7
D6
A-7
D6
(LAST x)

(MED.)

TWISTED

– WARDELL GRAY

TWO CIGARETTES IN THE DARK

(MED.)

-LEW POLLACK/PAUL FRANCIS WEBSTER

MED. (BLUES)

TWO DEGREES EAST, THREE DEGREES WEST

—JOHN LEWIS

UNTIL I MET YOU
(CORNER POCKET)
-FREDDIE GREEN/
DON WOLF
(MED. SWING)
Eb-7 Ab7 Db6 F-7 Bb7
Eb-7 Ab7 Db6
1. F-7 Bb7
2. (Db6)
Ab-7 Db7 Gbmaj7
Bb-7 Eb7 Ab7 Eb-7 Ab7
Eb-7 Ab7 Db6 F-7 Bb7
Eb-7 Ab7 Db6 (F-7 Bb7)

(MED.)

WALKIN' SHOES

– GERRY MULLIGAN

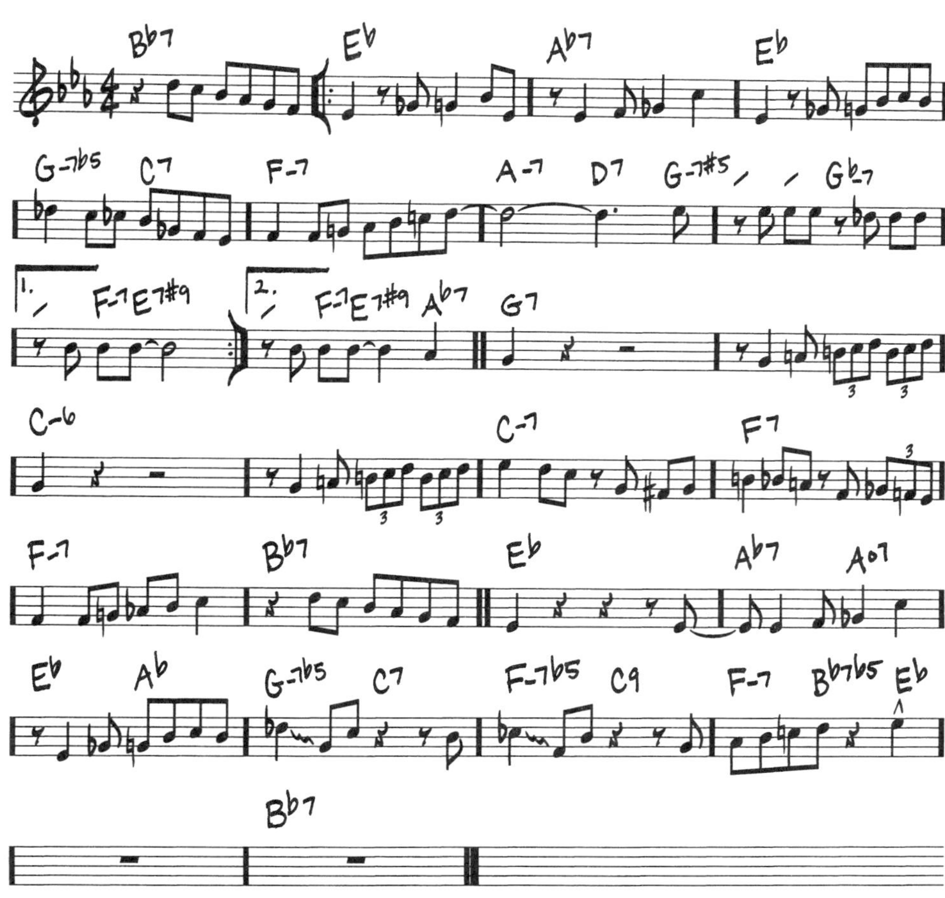

(MED.)

A WALKIN' THING

—BENNY CARTER

WARM VALLEY

(MED. BALLAD) — DUKE ELLINGTON

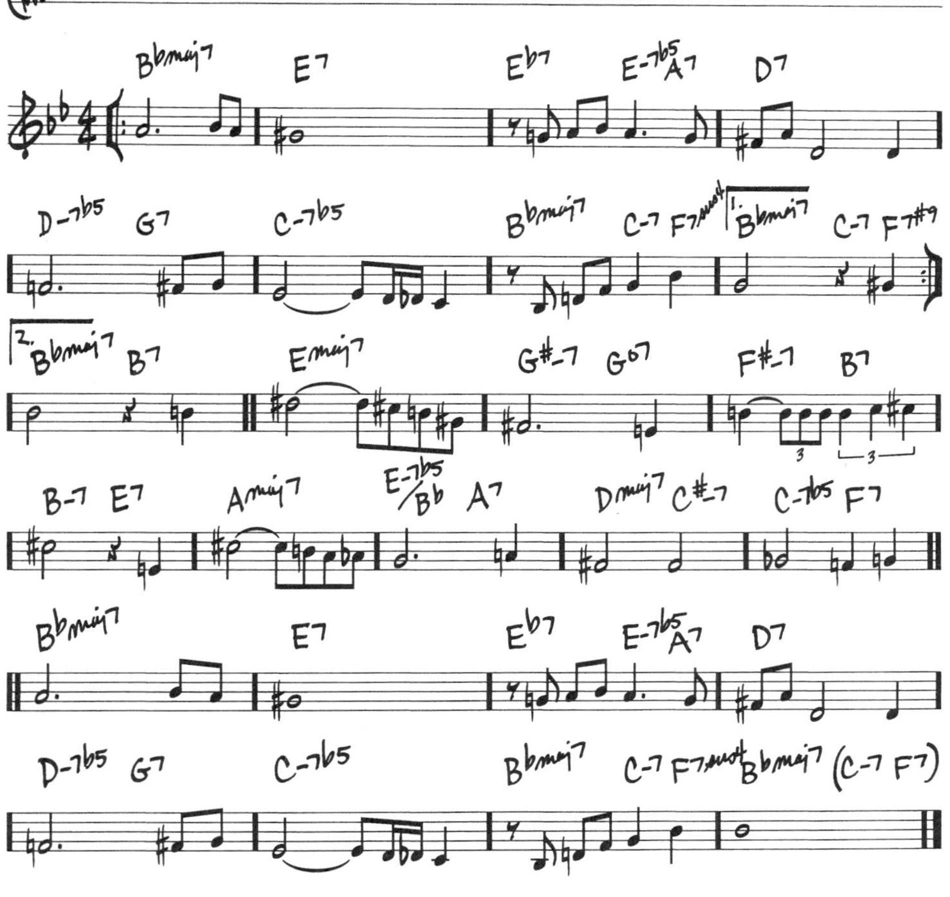

(Bossa)

WATCH WHAT HAPPENS

–MICHEL LEGRAND/JACQUES DEMY/NORMAN GIMBEL

WATER COLORS
—PAT METHENY
(♩=150 EVEN 8THS)
Ebmaj7 Bb9sus4 Db6/9
Cbmaj7#5
Ebmaj7 G7#5(#9) Dbmaj
Bb/C Cbmaj7 Gbmaj7 F/G
C-7 Db13 C-7
Bbmaj7 Ab/Bb F#/G#
Gmaj7
Gbmaj7 F-7
E6/9#11
A
G#-7
Gbmaj7 Db7/F
Cbmaj7/Eb Bb7b9/D
C-7 G-7/Bb
1.
Abmaj7
FINE
2.
Abmaj7
SOLOS
(0)
G-7
(PLAY 4x)
Dbmaj7
C-7
Bb-7 Eb7
OPEN
Bb-7 Eb7
LAST TIME
B-7 E7
AFTER SOLOS, D.C. AL FINE

MED. (OR BALLAD)

A WEAVER OF DREAMS

- VICTOR YOUNG/ JACK ELLIOTT

WEBB CITY
(MED. UP SWING)
– EARL "BUD" POWELL

(MED. SLOW)
WENDY
—PAUL DESMOND
Ebmaj7 C-7 F-7 Bb7
G-7 C7 Ab-7 Db7
1.
G-7 Gbo7 F-7 D-7b5 G7#5
C-7 F7 F-7 Bb7
2.
G-7 C7 A-7 D7 G7sus4 G7 C7
F-7 Bb7 Bmaj7 Emaj7
AFTER SOLOS, D.C. AL
Emaj7 Ebmaj7

(MED. LATIN)
WHAT A DIFF'RENCE A DAY MADE
- MARIA GREVER / STANLEY ADAMS
G-7 C7 Fmaj7 Bb9 A-7 Abo7
G-7 C7 Fmaj7
E-7 A7 D-7
G7 C7sus4 C7
G-7 C7 Fmaj7 Bb9 A-7 Abo7
G-7 C7 F9 C-7 F9
Bbmaj7 Eb9 Fmaj7 Abo7
G-7 C7 F6

WHAT A WONDERFUL WORLD

(BALLAD)

–GEORGE DAVID WEISS/BOB THIELE

(MED. BALLAD)

WHAT'S NEW?

– BOB HAGGART/
JOHNNY BURKE

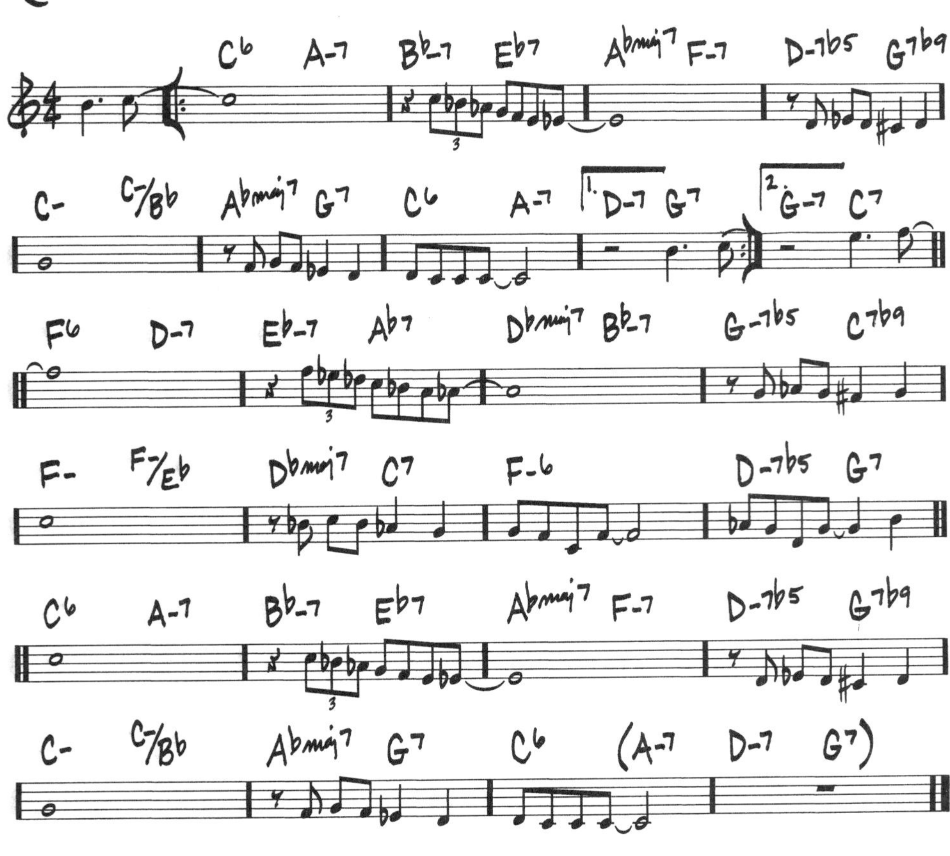

WHERE OR WHEN

– RICHARD RODGERS/
LORENZ HART

(MED.)

WHISPER NOT

(MED.)

— BENNY GOLSON

WHO CAN I TURN TO
(WHEN NOBODY NEEDS ME)

(MED. BALLAD)

- LESLIE BRICUSSE/
ANTHONY NEWLEY

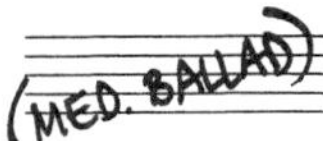

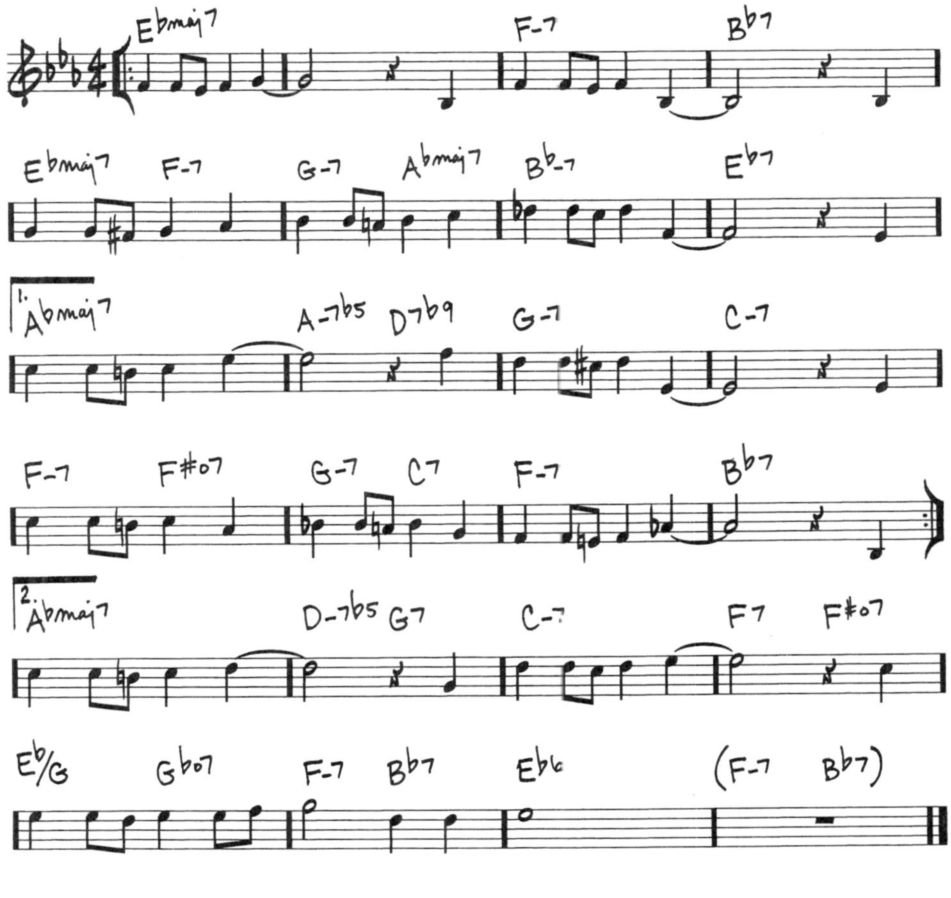
Ebmaj7 F-7 Bb7
Ebmaj7 F-7 G-7 Abmaj7 Bb-7 Eb7
1.
Abmaj7 A-7b5 D7b9 G-7 C-7
F-7 F#o7 G-7 C7 F-7 Bb7
2.
Abmaj7 D-7b5 G7 C-7 F7 F#o7
Eb/G Gbo7 F-7 Bb7 Eb6 (F-7 Bb7)

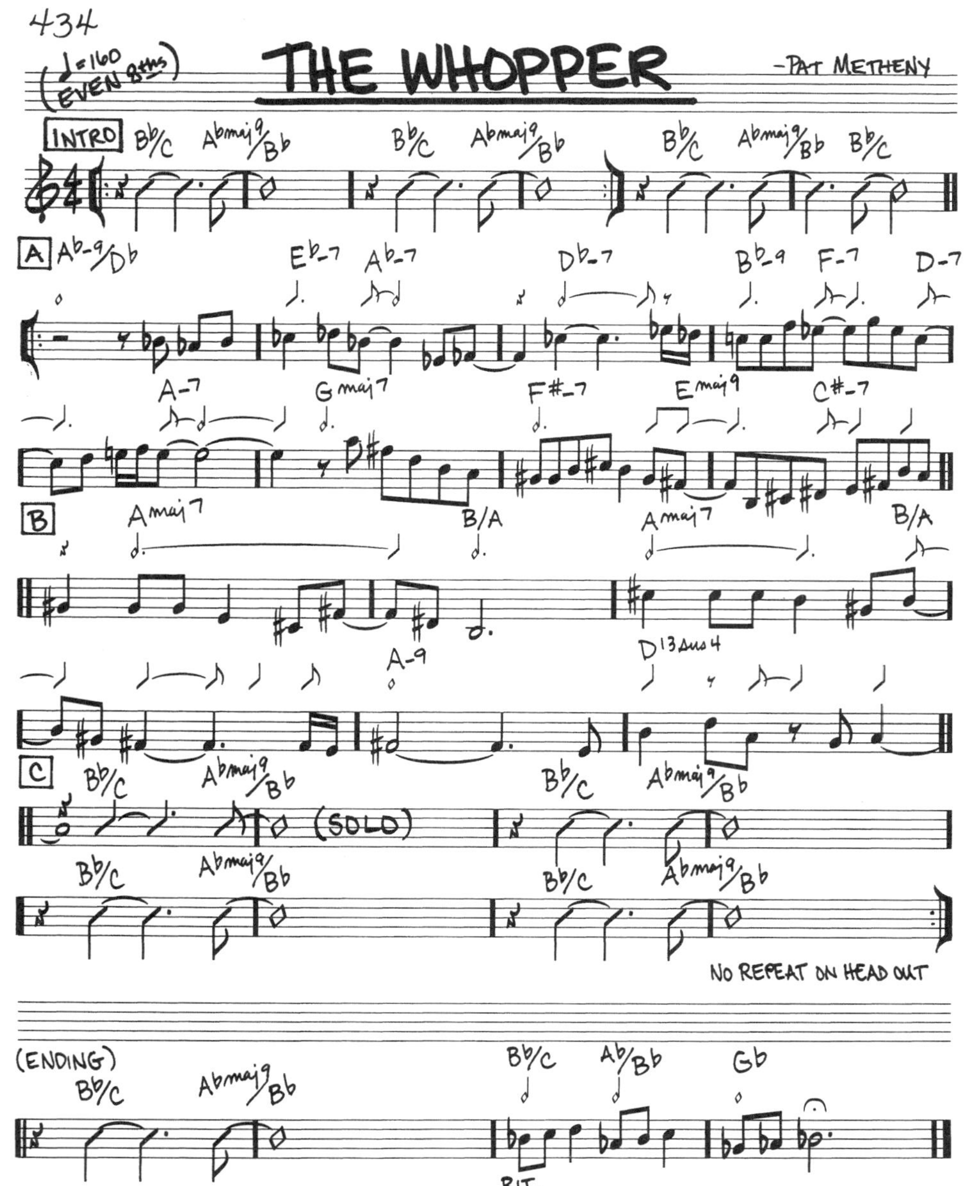

434
THE WHOPPER
-PAT METHENY
(♩=160 EVEN 8THS)
INTRO
Bb/C Abmaj9/Bb Bb/C Abmaj9/Bb Bb/C Abmaj9/Bb Bb/C
A
Ab-9/Db Eb-7 Ab-7 Db-7 Bb-9 F-7 D-7
A-7 Gmaj7 F#-7 Emaj9 C#-7
B
Amaj7 B/A Amaj7 B/A
A-9 D13sus4
C
Bb/C Abmaj9/Bb (SOLO) Bb/C Abmaj9/Bb
Bb/C Abmaj9/Bb Bb/C Abmaj9/Bb
NO REPEAT ON HEAD OUT
(ENDING)
Bb/C Abmaj9/Bb Bb/C Ab/Bb Gb
RIT.

WHY DO I LOVE YOU?

(MED.)

—JEROME KERN/OSCAR HAMMERSTEIN II

(UP)

WILL YOU STILL BE MINE

- MATT DENNIS/
TOM ADAIR

B7
Bb7#5(#9)
Bb-7
Eb7
Abmaj7
Db9(#11)
Eb6
C-7
F#-7
B7
F-7
Bb7
Ebmaj7
G-7
C7
F-7
Bb7
Ebmaj7
G-7
C7
F-7
D-7b5
G7
C-7
F7
F-7
Bb7
Eb6
(F-7 Bb7)

WITCHCRAFT

-Cy Coleman/
Carolyn Leigh

(MED.)

WITH A SONG IN MY HEART

- RICHARD RODGERS/ LORENZ HART

WITHOUT A SONG

(MED. FAST)

– WILLIAM ROSE/
EDWARD ELISCU/
VINCENT YOUMANS

YARDBIRD SUITE

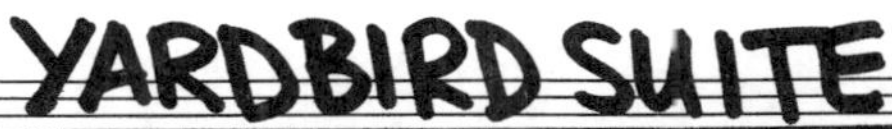

–CHARLIE PARKER

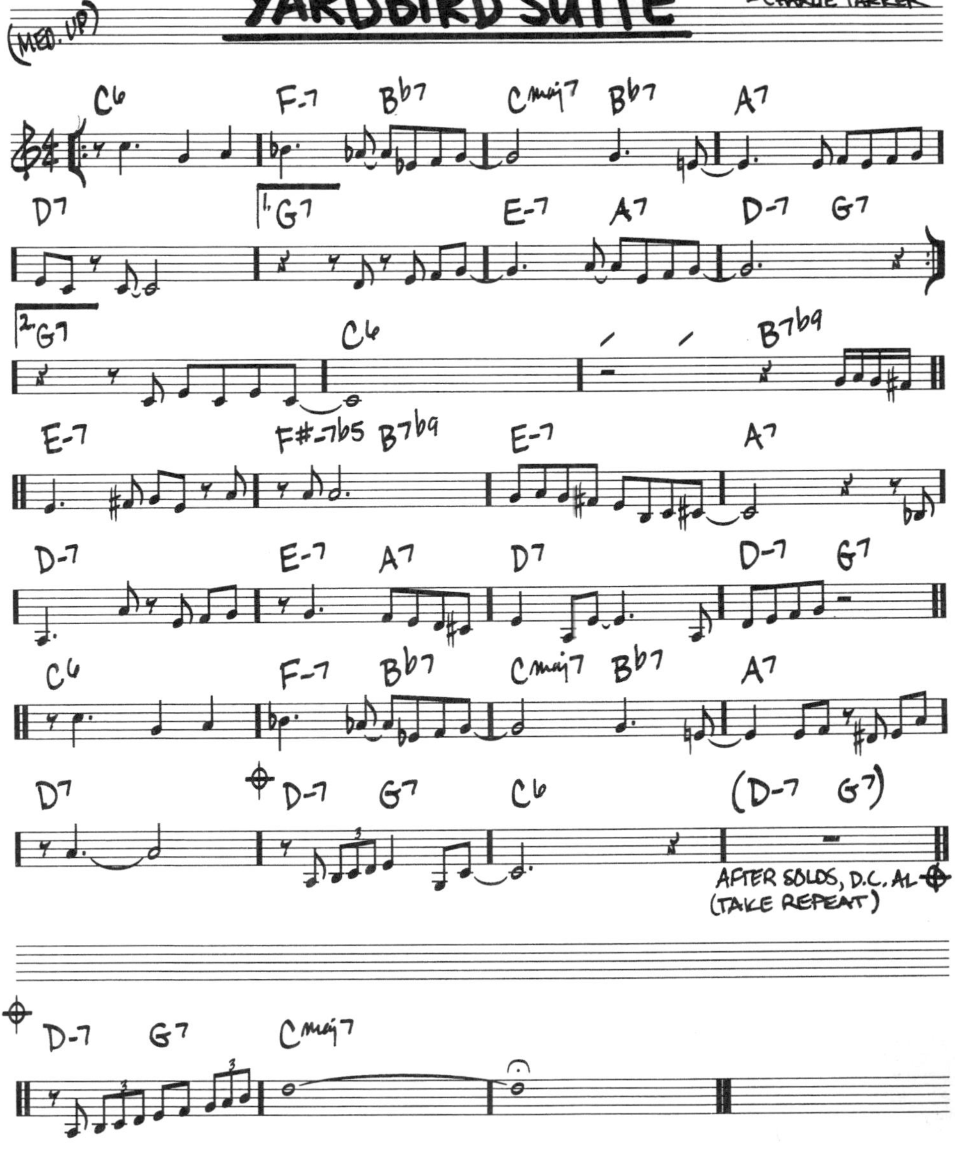
(MED. UP)
C6 F-7 Bb7 Cmaj7 Bb7 A7
D7 G7 E-7 A7 D-7 G7
G7 C6 B7b9
E-7 F#-7b5 B7b9 E-7 A7
D-7 E-7 A7 D7 D-7 G7
C6 F-7 Bb7 Cmaj7 Bb7 A7
D7 D-7 G7 C6 (D-7 G7)
AFTER SOLOS, D.C. AL
(TAKE REPEAT)
D-7 G7 Cmaj7

(Bright) A Wonderful Day Like Today

– Leslie Bricusse/Anthony Newley

Ebmaj7 Eb6 Ebmaj7 Eb6

Ebmaj7 Eb6 F–7 Bb7

F–7 Bb7 G–7 C7

1. Abmaj7 F7 F–7 Bb7

2. Abmaj7 F–7 Bb7 Eb6 F–7 F#o7 G7

Ab Ab+ Ab6 Ab7 Ao7

Ebmaj7 F–7 Bb7 Ebmaj7 Eb7

Abmaj7 A–7b5 D7b9

G–7 C7 F7 Bb7

Ebmaj7
Eb6
Ebmaj7
Eb6
Ebmaj7
Eb6
F-7
Bb7
F-7
Bb7
G-7
C7
Abmaj7
G7
C-7
F7
F-7
Bb7
Eb6
(F-7 Bb7)

YOU ARE BEAUTIFUL

(MED. BALLAD)

-RICHARD RODGERS/OSCAR HAMMERSTEIN II

YOU CAN DEPEND ON ME

(MED. FAST)

-CHARLES CARPENTER/LOUIS DUNLAP/EARL HINES

(MED.)

YOU'RE MY EVERYTHING

-HARRY WARREN/MORT DIXON/JOE YOUNG

(MED.) YOU'RE NOBODY 'TIL SOMEBODY LOVES YOU

—RUSS MORGAN/LARRY STOCK/JAMES CAVANAUGH